Robert J. Dixson

CB081818

Modern Short Stories

English

by American Authors

An Advanced Reader
with Exercises for Conversation
and Vocabulary Drill

DISAL
EDITORA

© 2007 Robert J. Dixson

Assistente editorial: Gabriela Canato

Capa: Alberto Mateus

Dados Internacionais de Catalogação na Publicação (CIP)
(Câmara Brasileira do Livro, SP, Brasil)

Modern short stories in English by American authors : an advanced reader / illustrations by Nancy Ward. -- Barueri, SP : DISAL, 2007.

Vários autores
ISBN 978-85-89533-87-4

1. Contos norte-americanos 2. Inglês - Livros-texto para estrangeiros I. Dixson, Robert James. II. Ward, Nancy.

07-9361 CDD-428

Índice para catálogo sistemático:
1. Inglês para brasileiros : Lingüística aplicada 428

DISAL EDITORA

Todos os direitos reservados em nome de:
Bantim, Canato e Guazzelli Editora Ltda.

Al. Mamoré, 911 - sala 107, Alphaville
06454-040, Barueri - SP
Tel./Fax: **55 11 4195-2811**

Visite nosso site: www.disaleditora.com.br

VENDAS
Televendas: (11) 3226-3111
Fax gratuito: 0800 7707 105/106
E-mail para pedidos: comercialdisal@disal.com.br

Nenhuma parte desta publicação pode ser reproduzida, arquivada ou transmitida de nenhuma forma ou meio sem permissão expressa e por escrito da Editora.

Preface

All the stories in this book have appeared in current magazines. They have been written by well-known authors and deal almost entirely with present-day American life. The stories should be of particular interest to the many students everywhere who, while studying English, wish at the same time to learn something of the American scene.

The stories have been adapted only slightly, and the book is designed for use by advanced students. Slang expressions and words of unusual difficulty have been eliminated, but otherwise the stories remain as originally written. No attempt has been made to alter in any way the style of the individual authors.

The stories fall within the form known today as the short short-story. Stories of this type were selected intentionally, as providing a very convenient study medium. Each story is only four or five pages in length and can be studied easily within one or two class sessions. Such a story, as any teacher will recognize, has a great advantage over the old fashioned short-story, which sometimes stretched itself over thirty or forty pages.

Each story is provided with study helps. There are vocabulary review exercises. There are also questions based on the story for conversational purposes. The teacher can easily expand upon these questions if more conversational material is required. A question like, "Why did not Mr. Whitney call the police?" can be supplemented with "What did Mr. Whitney do instead of calling the police?" "What would you have done in Mr. Whitney's situation?" etc. Each question can thus lead to other questions and to interesting and lively class discussions as well.

The present reader is one of a series of three readers for foreign students prepared by the author. The first, entitled *Elementary Reader* is a book of simple reading selections for the beginning student. The second, *Easy Reading Selections* is for use on the intermediate level. This book, as mentioned above, is for the advanced student. If the material in this book proves to be too difficult for some classes, it is suggested that one of the two easier readers be tried. For a grammar supplement to this book, if such is indicated, the author's *Graded Exercises in English for the Foreign Born* is suggested.

R. J. D.

CONTENTS

BEST LOOKING GIRL IN TOWN

Thyra Samter Winslow

Best Looking Girl in Town

Thyra Samter Winslow

From the time she was thirteen Rilla Mabry had been ashamed of her appearance. It was then that she started growing taller than the other girls. She was also awkward as well as tall and she was too thin.

By the time she was twenty she was fully convinced that her appearance was really something terrible. All of the other girls seemed little and cute and attractive. No matter what Rilla wore it seemed wrong. She was much too tall to wear tailored clothes. And thin dresses simply hung around her loosely.

All of the boys and girls in the group liked Rilla. She was a fine girl—if you could forget the way she looked. Even her hair was wrong—rather stringy—but she had a pleasant and rather attractive face.

In spite of her looks Rilla had a boy friend. He was Patrick Redding and his father kept a grocery store. Pat wasn't any great prize—but then you couldn't expect Rilla, with her looks, to do any better. People felt that Rilla ought to be well satisfied. Pat was a nice looking boy, and he shouldn't be considered unimportant.

Rilla didn't consider Pat unimportant. She was grateful to him for being nice to her. She was as pleasant and as friendly as she could be. As a matter of fact she liked Pat a lot. He was fun to be with. She would have been perfectly satisfied except for the fact that she was in love with Shane Tennant. All of which did her little good—for Shane was the prize of the town. Shane's father was a banker—and rich. His mother was the social leader of the town. Shane was tall—much taller than Rilla—and handsome, besides.

Pat went into the grocery business with his father. Shane went into the bank. That's the way sons do in small towns unless they have definite ideals about law or one of the other professions. Rilla didn't do anything. Her parents had just enough money so she didn't have to work. She went to parties with Patrick—and admired Shane from a distance. The town people felt that she would marry Pat, that he'd take over his father's grocery store and that they'd settle down.

That might have happened if it hadn't been for Leslie Durant. Leslie Durant was—and still is—a well known magazine illustrator. And he came to Morrisville to visit an aunt. And he was taken everywhere to all of the parties, of course. He was the social lion of the season. He stayed in town for only a few days—but that was long enough for a lot to happen.

He saw Rilla Mabry! Rilla was standing near the door—and she was looking at Shane Tennant. She never knew how much her face showed what she was thinking about. No one else noticed—but Durant, being new, understood the situation. He saw Rilla, standing not quite straight because she didn't feel quite as tall that way, in a badly fitted dress and her hair not quite smooth—and he saw Shane, perfectly dressed, self-confident, good-looking. And then Pat came to ask Rilla to dance.

On the second day of his visit Durant made his remarkable statement. He told anyone who would listen to him that Rilla Mabry was by far the best looking girl in town. One of the best looking girls he had ever seen.

Rilla had never had a compliment about her looks before. She had always been shy, self-conscious, and often unhappy about her appearance. And now, the first authority on beauty who had ever been in town claimed that she was the prize.

When Durant, himself, told her what he thought of her she was filled with confusion. She managed finally to thank him. And later, very shyly, she went up to him.

"I do wish that you'd tell me how I can look better," she said.

"That's not really my particular kind of work," he told her, "but maybe if we got together. . . ."

They got together the next morning. Durant came to Rilla's house, and, with Rilla's mother acting as helper, they did things to Rilla and to Rilla's clothes. Durant made her stand up straight. And he rearranged her hair. And he told her what was wrong with the clothes she wore.

That night there was a dance for Durant—his last evening in town. And, as he had thought when he started things, Rilla was, for the first time in her life, the center of attention. Toward the end of the evening Durant had the satisfaction of seeing Shane Tennant dancing very attentively with Rilla, Shane Tennant, whom Rilla had looked at with longing eyes—and who had never paid any attention to her.

Durant went back to his home and his work in New York. And forgot about the whole thing. And years passed. And then, just the other day, this happened:

Durant was lunching alone at a restaurant when an attractive, tall woman, past her first youth, came up to him.

"You don't remember me?" she said.

Durant didn't remember her.

"I'm Rilla Tennant—I was Rilla Mabry when you knew me. You came to my home town and—and rather made my life over. Remember now?"

"Of course I do," said Durant. "I remember very well. It was my one attempt at changing the destiny of another person."

"You did a wonderful job!" said Rilla. There was a strange note in her voice which he didn't understand.

"You married the boy you were in love with, I see. His name was Tennant, wasn't it?"

"Why, yes," said Rilla. "But how did you remember the name? And how did you know I was in love with him?"

"I'm good at remembering names. And I saw you looking at him. Simplicity itself! And to think that I was the cause!"

"Yes, you were," said Rilla. "It was very funny, when you look back on it. There I was, going with Pat Redding and in love with Shane, and terribly unhappy and awkward. And you came down and said I was a beauty—so automatically I became a beauty. And the boys all wanted to go out with me. And I married Shane."

"Wonderful!" said Durant. And he smiled happily. "How are you getting along, now?"

"That's the difficult part," said Rilla. "You shouldn't have asked.

"Shane and I got married—and didn't get along very well, though I was awfully happy in the beginning. The Tennants lost all of their money in a bank failure—and my family had its money in the Tennant bank by that time, so our money went, too. Then Shane fell in love with a chorus girl. I got a divorce, of course. I've been teaching in a girl's school for the past three years."

"That's too bad!" said Durant. "But maybe that was better than marrying that other boy whom you didn't love."

"Maybe," said Rilla. "You can never tell. Love goes. . . . Patrick Redding took over his father's grocery store—and married the cutest girl in town. They have three children and are very happy. And, oh yes, he became quite ambitious and started a chain of grocery stores. Now he's the richest and most important man in town."

Exercises for Conversation

A—Answer these Questions:

1. Why had Rilla Mabry, as a young girl, been ashamed of her appearance? 2. Had she grown taller or shorter than the other girls? 3. Why did people think that Rilla ought to be well satisfied with Pat Redding as a boy friend? 4. With whom was Rilla in love at the time? 5. Why did Rilla, as a girl, always have to admire Shane Tennant at a distance? 6. Who was Leslie Durant and why did he come to Morrisville at this time? 7. Why was he the "social lion" of the season? 8. What did Durant say about Rilla Mabry when he first saw her? 9. Why was Durant considered an authority on the question of beauty? 10. What suggestions did Durant make to Rilla about changing her appearance? 11. Whom did Rilla finally marry? 12. How did Rilla's marriage with Shane Tennant turn out? 13. Whom did Pat Redding, Rilla's first boy friend, finally marry? 14. How did Pat Redding become the richest and most important man in town?

B—Give Sentences with the Following:

to be ashamed of	to settle down
to be in love with	by far
to take over	to manage to do something

to go (come) up to
to get together
to make something over
to get along
to get married
to be too bad

C—Vocabulary Practice: Answer the following correctly:

1. Which *two* of the following words are used as opposites of *thin* (thick, bright, light, fat, grateful)?

2. What is the past tense form of these verbs: to hang, to wear, to grow, to do, to forget?

3. Which of the following do you buy in a grocery store (nails, dresses, food, clothes)?

4. To *take over* something is to (reject it, desire it, assume control of it, claim it).

5. What is the verb form of the noun *illustrator?* What is the difference between an illustrator and an illustration?

6. If my *aunt* is my mother's sister, what do I call my mother's brother?

7. Which of these is the opposite of *straight* (beautiful, crooked, definite, self-conscious)?

8. Which of these is the opposite of *awkward* (graceful, tall, stringy, satisfied)?

9. A man who is handsome may also be said to be (rich, homely, shy, good-looking)?

10. Which of these is the opposite of *ambitious* (timid, lazy, unhappy, self-confident)?

11. On which syllable do we accent each of these words: situation, conscious, profession, grocery?

12. What meaning does the prefix *re* give to each of the following: rearrange, remake, remodel?

TO LOVE AND TO HONOR

Octavus Roy Cohen

To Love and to Honor

Octavus Roy Cohen

It was rather surprising to discover a deep vein of sentiment in little George Potter. I had been his friend and his lawyer for many years and had watched the always fat, and once alert, little man settle into a domestic routine. He had been moderately successful in business, sufficiently successful to permit him to retire from business and to travel about the world a little if he had wanted to do so. But instead he and Esther were content to sit night after night in their pleasant living-room; she busy with her sewing or reading; he passing the time with his very excellent collection of postage-stamps.

Looking back over the years of my friendship with Potter, I can see that the vein of romance had probably been there all the time. There was, for instance, his very romantic love-affair with Althea Deane—an affair which almost became a scandal. But just when people began to gossip about them, George married her.

That marriage appeared to extinguish George Potter's last spark of romanticism. It never had a chance to be successful, and when Althea left him suddenly, George's friends considered that he was fortunate to lose her. Later came the news of Althea's death while living abroad, and a couple of years later George began to call upon Esther seriously. The people of our group were only slightly interested—it is difficult to become greatly excited over a possible marriage when both the man and the woman are equally rather dull and uninteresting.

The marriage was a very nice affair. There followed the usual series of parties for the newly married couple. Then it seemed that George and Esther retired from life. Even his business affairs ran so well that there was little need on George's part for my services as his lawyer—and while I never ceased to like him, we found less and less in common as the years passed. I couldn't imagine that they were happy; perhaps they were contented, but not really happy. There wasn't enough sentiment. . . . That's the way I figured George. And nothing happened to change my opinion until a few weeks before their twenty-fifth anniversary.

It was then that he came into my office, his fat little face shining with enthusiasm, and told me of his unusual plans for the silver anniversary. His bright little eyes shone as he explained the thing, and I'll confess that I was pretty well confused; not alone because his plan was very sentimental and profoundly impressive; but mainly because it was quiet, dull, old George Potter who was planning this thing—the very George Potter who had lived a quiet life since his second marriage, and who had avoided social contacts.

According to what George told me, he was doing this thing for Esther's sake. "It'll please her," he explained. "Women like that sort of thing, you know—and this seems to me a real idea. You have to be a part of it, because you were best man when Esther and I were married. It's just a gesture on my part—a sort of sacrifice to please the Old Lady."

I'll say this for George; he didn't do things halfway. Instead of the usual party, he presented a perfect duplication of his marriage to Esther twenty-five years before. There was even the same minister—very old now—and the same violinist who had played "Oh, Promise Me" at the other ceremony. A good many of the original guests were there: most of us rather gray-haired now. But the thing was very impressive: Esther in the same bridal dress she had worn twenty-five years before—let out around the hips perhaps—and carrying a bouquet of bride roses, the bridesmaids in pink, with bouquets of Killarney roses; even a person to carry the ring. It was great fun and very impressive where one might have expected it to be absurd.

As for Esther, I never saw a woman look more beautiful. She took on an aura of genuine beauty. Of course she would have been less than human and far from feminine to have failed to respond to this magnificent exhibition of husbandly devotion. George himself was as frightened as he had been on the occasion of their first wedding.

But finally the ceremony was finished and the guests went to the dining-room for the rich supper which had been prepared by special cooks employed for the occasion. George and I were left alone and he sank exhausted into a chair. I placed my hand on his shoulder and congratulated him on the success of his party.

"You really think it was a success?"

"Wonderful! And," jokingly, "you certainly should feel completely married."

"Yes, I do." He became silent for a moment or two, and when he spoke again it was in a deeply serious tone. "There's something I've got to explain to you: as my friend and my lawyer." He stopped for a second, then asked suddenly, "You remember my first wife?"

"Althea?" I was surprised by the question. "Certainly."

"Did you know," he went on in a strange voice, "that she died only last year?"

"Good Lord! I thought she died twenty-seven years ago."

"So did I," he said quietly. "And when I married Esther, I thought I was a widower. But I wasn't—and in case anything ever comes up—well, I want you to understand that this affair tonight was a real wedding for Esther and me."

Exercises for Conversation

A—Answer these Questions:

1. By whom is this story told? 2. How did George Potter and his wife Esther pass the time night after night in their pleasant living room? 3. Was George Potter a poor man or was he moderately rich? 4. How did George Potter's first marriage with Althea Deane terminate? 5. Why were the people of the community little interested in the possible marriage of George Potter with Esther, whom he now began to call upon? 6. Did George and Esther, after their marriage, lead a very active social life or did they seem to retire from life? 7. Why did George Potter have little need for the services of his lawyer as the years went on? 8. What plans did George Potter make for his twenty-fifth wedding anniversary? 9. Why did these plans seem very unusual to his lawyer friend, who tells this story? 10. For whose sake, according to George, was he doing this thing? 11. Why did George ask his lawyer friend to be best man at the wedding ceremony? 12. Was the wedding party a simple or an elaborate affair? 13. What minister and what violinist took part in the ceremony? 14. Was the whole affair very impressive or did it appear a little absurd?

15. What, according to what George Potter told his friend later, was the real explanation for this second wedding?

B—Give Sentences with the Following:

to do so	in common
night after night	to do something halfway
to pass the time	to let something out
to call upon	as for
to become excited over	in case
to run well	to come up

C—Vocabulary Practice. Answer the following correctly:

1. We generally buy stamps in a (book-store, post-office, movie, grocery).
2. Which of the following words can be used both as a noun and a verb without any change in form (scandal, marriage, gossip, excellent)?
3. Which of these words is not spelled correctly (difficult, sentiment, anniversery, impressive).
4. Which of the following words often means the same as *uninteresting* (dull, bright, silver, social)?
5. *To cease* means (to begin, to avoid, to duplicate, to stop).
6. A common synonym for *unusual* is (new, strange, uninteresting, old).
7. Which of the following are adverbs (sentimental, impressively, newly, contented, profoundly)?
8. On which syllable do we accent the following words: impressive, bouquet, original, feminine?
9. A bridesmaid generally carries a (bride, purse, bouquet, ring).
10. If a widow is a woman whose husband has died, what do we call a man whose wife has died?
11. What is the past tense form of these verbs: to carry, to do, to leave, to congratulate, to let, to present, to confuse, to imagine?
12. The opposite of *genuine* is (big, alone, exhausted, false).

JOHN ROSSITER'S WIFE

Charles G. Norris

John Rossiter's Wife

Charles G. Norris

The most fascinating place in the United States today, I consider, is Palm Beach and the most interesting spot in it is "Whitney's." The name isn't Whitney's at all, but anyone who has ever been to Palm Beach will know the establishment to which I refer.

Whitney's is a restaurant and a gambling place, and sooner or later everybody who comes to Palm Beach visits Whitney's.

There is no restaurant or hotel in France, Italy, Germany or Spain that can compare with Whitney's in the matter of food! At Whitney's there are no menus; you order what you wish from an endless variety of special foods, anything from duck soup to bird's tongues—and the surprising fact is that you get what you order. But on your first visit to Whitney's you often pay little attention to what you eat, for very soon, as the room commences to fill, you can hardly believe your eyes. At every table you soon recognize someone who is either famous or notorious.

After lunch this brilliantly dressed group of persons goes down to the gambling room. By two o'clock this room is well filled, by three it is crowded, and it remains so until the early hours of the morning. It is far more interesting and better conducted than Monte Carlo. I was deeply impressed, and soon I welcomed an opportunity to meet Mr. Whitney himself.

We found him in a small, businesslike office hardly

large enough to hold the big old-fashioned roll-top desk and a chair or two. Perhaps there was a safe; I can't remember. The office was protected by some iron bars, and there was a uniformed attendant at the door who admitted us after Mr. Whitney had given the word he would see us.

I found him a man square of jaw, cold of eye, his face rather unexpressive—much what I expected. He runs his gambling place as a business—and it is a matter of pride with him that it is conducted in an efficient, businesslike way. It is said that his profits are two million dollars a season, and I doubt this just as one doubts the salaries of motion picture stars.

However, the man had strong a personality. He interested me. I liked him. I wanted to talk to him, but it was difficult. He was not a very communicative person. Soon I asked him how much he lost a season in the way of bad checks and bad debts. He said approximately two hundred thousand dollars, which he didn't seem to consider as heavy. As he spoke of this a light came into his eyes, and a faint smile appeared on his lips.

"I had a rather interesting experience the other day," he said. "I was sitting in my office one morning when word was brought to me that a lady wanted to see me; 'Mrs. John Rossiter,' the man told me. I knew who John Rossiter was, so I told him to show her in.

"Before she said a word she began to cry, not bitterly; but the tears came into her eyes and began to run down her cheeks, and she kept wiping them away with her handkerchief, trying all the time to control herself. I don't like that sort of thing, you know, and I usually avoid it, but this rather impressed me. I felt sorry for her before she opened her mouth.

"Her husband had been gambling, she told me, and

on Wednesday—the day before—had lost thirty thousand dollars. I've been acquainted with John Rossiter off and on for five or six years. Every year he has been coming down here, and I've known him well enough to say 'Hello,' but not much more intimately than that. At any rate, I've always had a good feeling about Rossiter. He was a clean-cut man, a good sport, and was pretty well liked, belonged to a good club, and was rather popular everywhere. I had seen him year after year here, but I hadn't an idea of how he played or what he won or lost. He had an account with me and always paid very promptly at the end of the month if there was any paying to be done.

"Mrs. Rossiter explained that the great problem of her life had been her husband's gambling. She had begged him to keep away from the stock market and from cards, and he'd promise her that he'd stop, but then he'd slip and get caught again. The thirty thousand dollars he had lost on Wednesday about cleaned him and his wife out. It meant—oh, I've forgotten what she told me exactly: selling the home—it was mortgaged already, she said, taking the two girls out of school; herself perhaps having to find a position. It was a long story, I don't remember the details, but I confess that I felt very sorry for her. Taking those two girls out of school was what I believe impressed me, I don't know why exactly. Well, at any rate, I told her that I didn't like the idea of anybody coming here and losing everything. Sentiment, if you like, but it's good business at the same time. It doesn't help an establishment like this to get a reputation that people can lose everything they have here. The result of it all was that I agreed to give her back the money which her husband had lost, but on one condition, and I made that point very clear: John Rossiter was never to enter my place again. I don't like that kind of a 'loser' around here. If he hasn't got the money, he oughtn't to play. She promised me with the tears running down her cheeks, and I gave her the money, and she made me feel like a damn fool by kissing both my hands, and asking God to bless me—all that foolishness that a grateful woman feels she has to do when you do her a favor.

"I didn't think anything more about the affair until the very next afternoon when it was clearly brought back to my mind. My floor manager came to me and told me that John Rossiter had just come in, had gone to the gambling room, and was playing at one of the tables. As a rule, I never mix up with what happens outside, but this made me pretty mad, so I walked out there myself.

"I went straight up to him and said: 'May I speak to you a minute?' And when we were off in a corner away from the crowd, I asked him what he meant by coming into my place.

" 'I want to know what this means,' I demanded. 'Your wife came to see me yesterday morning and told me about your troubles and about your losing thirty thousand dollars here on Wednesday, and I gave her back the money you'd lost on one condition and that was that you were never to enter my doors again. Now, what do you mean by coming here?'

"Rossiter looked at me for a moment. Then he said:

" 'Why, Mr. Whitney, there must be some mistake. *I'm not married.*' "

Exercises for Conversation

A—Answer these Questions:

1. Where does the above story take place? 2. Was "Whitney's" a very simple or a very elaborate restaurant and gambling place? 3. Did many or few famous people visit Whitney's? 4. What kind of office did Mr. Whitney himself occupy? 5. Were the profits which Mr. Whitney made in one season very small or very large? 6. Why does the author say that Mr. Whitney appeared to be more or less the type of man that he expected to see? 7. Was Mr. Whitney a rather communicative or a rather uncommunicative man? 8. What woman had come to see Mr. Whitney recently? 9. Why did the woman begin to cry before telling Mr. Whitney her story? 10. Did "Mrs. Rossiter" say that her husband had lost much money or little money the day before? 11. What, according to her, had been the great problem of her life? 12. Why would she and Mr. Rossiter now have to sell their home, take their two daughters out of school, etc.? 13. What did Mr. Whitney finally agree to do? 14. What one condition, however, did he make before returning the money to her? 15. Why did Mr. Whitney become very angry the next day when he learned that Mr. Rossiter was again gambling in his place? 16. What did he say to Mr. Rossiter? How did Mr. Rossiter answer him?

B—Give Sentences with the Following:

at all
sooner or later
to pay attention to
to keep doing something
to show someone in (out)
to feel sorry for
to get acquainted with
at any rate
to get caught
to give back
as a rule

C—Vocabulary Practice. Answer the following correctly:

1. Which of these do we use in a restaurant (desk, safe, menu, season)?

2. The most famous gambling place in the world is located at (Washington, London, Venice, Monte Carlo).

3. A common synonym for the word *opportunity* is (hardly, chance, fame, surprise).

4. The best place in which to keep money is a (safe, gambling house, handkerchief, desk).

5. What is the adjective form of the noun *pride?*

6. What are the past tense forms of these verbs: to sit, to bring, to try, to control, to gamble, to be, to beg?

7. Which of the following words is not spelled correctly: detailed, controled, acquainted, begged?

8. With which of the following words does the contraction *he'd* rhyme: bed, led, seed, laid?

9. Which two of the following words may be used as the opposite of *to lose* (to gamble, to win, to wait, to find, to happen)?

10. If I am *pretty* mad, I am (awfully mad, not mad at all, rather mad).

11. What are the opposites of the following words: enter, outside, lose, loose, straight, bitter.

12. What is the noun form of the adjective *fascinating?*

A CASE OF SUSPICION

Ed Wallace

A Case of Suspicion

Ed Wallace

He threw back the covers and sat up on his bed, his feet feeling along the cold floor for his house slippers, the telephone ringing insistently a little distance away.

He turned on the light and walked to the phone, took down the receiver.

"This is Doctor Benson," he said.

The November wind was bringing sounds of winter as it blew around the little white house. The doctor got into his clothes. He went to the table and stared a moment at his watch, his spirit complaining at the job ahead of him.

Two o'clock. His mind also complained at the horrible hour and he wondered why children always had to be born at such improper times. He took up two small handbags, the short pill bag as the people of the town knew it, and the long obstetrical case, the baby bag they called it.

Doctor Benson stopped a moment to light a cigarette, then put the pack of cigarettes in his overcoat pocket. The wind felt like a surgeon's knife at his face as he opened the door and ran, bending low, around the driveway to the garage.

His car started with difficulty, coughed a half dozen times as he drove down the driveway but then began to run more smoothly as he turned down Grass Street and on to the deserted highway.

Mrs. Ott Sorley, whom Doctor Benson was on his way to visit, already had almost a dozen children, but it seemed to the doctor that never once had she had a baby in good weather, nor in daylight. And while Doctor Benson was a country doctor, he was still a young man and couldn't find the pleasure that his father, "the old Doc Benson" had found in seeing Ott, the father, always two or three babies behind in the payment of his baby bills.

It was a long ride out to the Sorley farm and the sight of a man walking alone along the country road, as seen just ahead by the lights of the car, was a welcome relief to the doctor. He slowed down and looked at the man walking along with difficulty against the wind, a little package under his arm.

Coming alongside, Doctor Benson stopped and invited the man to ride. The man got in.

"Are you going far?" asked the doctor.

"I'm going all the way to Detroit," said the man, a rather thin man with small black eyes filled with tears from the wind. "Could you give me a cigarette?"

Doctor Benson unbuttoned his coat, then remembered the cigarettes in the outer pocket of his overcoat. He took out the package and gave it to the rider who then looked in his own pockets for a match. When the cigarette was lighted, the man held the package a moment, then asked, "Do you mind, mister, if I take another cigarette for later?" The rider shook the package to remove another cigarette without waiting for the doctor to answer. Doctor Benson felt a hand touch his pocket.

"I'll put them back in your pocket," the little fellow said. Doctor Benson put his hand down quickly to receive the cigarettes and was a little irritated to find them already in his pocket.

After a few minutes Doctor Benson said: "So you're going to Detroit?"

"I'm going out to look for work in one of the automobile plants."

"Are you a mechanic?" asked the doctor.

"More or less. I've been driving a truck since the war ended. But I lost my job about a month ago."

"Were you in the army during the war?"

"Yeah, I was in the ambulance section. Right up at the front. Drove an ambulance for four years."

"Is that so?" said Doctor Benson. "I'm a doctor myself. Doctor Benson is my name."

"I thought this car smelled like pills," the man laughed. Then he added, more seriously, "My name is Evans."

They rode along silently for a few minutes and the rider moved himself in his seat and placed his package on the floor. As the man leaned over, Doctor Benson caught his first good look at the small, catlike face.

The doctor also noticed the long deep scar on the man's cheek, bright and red-looking as though it were of recent origin. He thought of Mrs. Ott Sorley and reached for his watch. His fingers went deep into his pocket before he realized that his watch was not there.

Doctor Benson moved his hand very slowly and very carefully below the seat until he felt the leather holster in which he always carried with him his automatic pistol.

He drew out the pistol slowly and held it in the darkness at his side. Doctor Benson stopped the car quickly and pushed the nose of his gun into Evans' side.

"Put that watch into my pocket," he said angrily.

The rider jumped with fear and put up his hands quickly. "My God, mister," he whispered, "I thought you. . . ."

Doctor Benson pushed the pistol still deeper into the

man's side and repeated coldly, "Put that watch in my pocket before I let this gun go off."

Evans put his hand in his own vest pocket and later, with trembling hands, tried to put the watch into the doctor's pocket. With his free hand Doctor Benson pushed the watch down into his pocket. He opened the door and forced the man out of the car.

"I'm out here tonight, probably to save a woman's life, but I took the time to try to help you," he said to the man angrily.

Doctor Benson started the car quickly and the wind closed the door with a loud noise. He put the pistol back into the leather holster under the seat and hurried on.

The drive up the mountain to the Sorley farm was less difficult than he had feared and Ott Sorley had sent one of his older boys down the road with a lantern to help him across the old wooden bridge that led up to the little farm house.

Mrs. Sorley's many previous experiences with bringing children into the world apparently helped her greatly because she delivered this child with little difficulty and there was no need on Doctor Benson's part for the instruments in the long bag.

After it was all over, however, Doctor Benson took out a cigarette and sat down to smoke.

"A fellow I picked up in my car on my way up here tonight tried to rob me," he said to Ott, feeling a little proud. "He took my watch. But when I pushed my .45 pistol into his side he decided to give it to me back."

Ott smiled wide at such an exciting story coming from young Doctor Benson.

"Well, I'm glad he gave it to you back," Ott said. "Because if he hadn't, we wouldn't have any idea what time the child was born. What time would you say it happened, Doc?"

Doctor Benson took the watch from his pocket.

"The baby was delivered about thirty minutes ago, and right now it's . . ." He walked over to the lamp on the table.

He stared strangely at the watch in his hand. The crystal was cracked, the top was broken. He turned the watch over and held it closer to the lamp. He studied the worn inscription there:

"To Private T. Evans, Ambulance Section, whose personal bravery preserved our lives the night of Nov. 3, 1943, near the Italian front. Nurses Nesbitt, Jones and Wingate."

Exercises for Conversation

A—Answer the Following:

1. At approximately what time of night was Doctor Benson awakened by the ringing of the telephone? 2. Who was calling him at this hour? 3. Does this story take place on a cold, windy night or on a warm summer night? 4. Was this Mrs. Sorley's first child or had she had many children previously? 5. In what kind of weather and at what hours did it seem to Doctor Benson that Mrs. Sorley always had her children? 6. Whom did Doctor Benson see walking ahead of him along the lonely country road? 7. Why was it a relief to the doctor to see someone along this road? 8. To what city did the man whom the doctor picked up say that he was going? 9. In what section of the army did the man say that he had been stationed? 10. What features of the man's appearance made Doctor Benson a little suspicious of him? 11. When Doctor Benson discovered that his watch was not in his pocket what did he reach for under the seat? 12. What did he say to the man as he pushed the gun into his side? 13. To whom did Doctor Benson later tell his story about the man he had picked

up along the road? 14. Why did Mr. Sorley say that he was very glad that the man had returned the watch to Doctor Benson? 15. After examining the watch, what inscription did Doctor Benson find on the back?

B—Give Sentences with the Following:

to sit up	to look for
to turn on	more or less
on his way to	to drive a car (truck)
to slow down	to lean over
to take out	to reach for
to put something back	to be over

C—Vocabulary Practice. Answer each of the following correctly:

1. If a telephone rings *insistently,* it rings (off and on, seldom, now and then, steadily).

2. When we are sick the doctor sometimes gives us (slippers, pills, pistols, cigarettes).

3. When we say that "he picked up the *receiver*", we are generally referring to a part of (a doctor's handbag, a cigarette case, a telephone, a farmyard).

4. What is the difference between a *doctor* and a *surgeon?*

5. Which of these do we generally wear only in the wintertime (slippers, overcoat, vest, stockings)?

6. Which of these is a common synonym for the word *automobile* (car, truck, plane, case)?

7. Which of these words is not spelled correctly (ceiling, releif, cigarette, exciting)?

8. If you lose something you generally (look at it, look it up, look it over, look for it).

9. Which of these is best able to repair the motor of your automobile (farmer, truck-driver, druggist, mechanic)?

10. When I say that the lesson is *over,* I mean that it has (begun, been interesting, been cancelled, ended).

11. What two different meanings does the word *plant* have in English today?

12. Which of these will help you to see in the dark (pistol, holster, watch, lantern)?

CLOCKWORK

Howard Breslin

Clockwork

Howard Breslin

It was a small window with narrow pieces of paper pasted across it to prevent its breaking during the heavy air raids. In the small space at the center that remained, a little man with eyeglasses was carefully setting out his display of clocks and watches. He paid no attention to the many Londoners hurrying by to begin another day.

When he finished placing his merchandise, the little man came out of the shop and stared in the window. He had placed the clocks and watches with great care—the clocks in a row at the back, and in front of them lying flat, a semi-circle of watches. All the clocks had their faces neatly divided in the middle by hands that pointed to six o'clock; all the watches, thin or fat, had their hands pointing straight at three o'clock.

"Yes," said the jeweler with a satisfied look. "Very nice."

About an hour later a passenger got out of the bus at the corner. He was a tall man with a blonde moustache, and he wore a heavy overcoat and a black hat. He was slightly lame and carried a cane. He smiled when the policeman at the corner said "Good morning" to him. The lame man's name was Gebhardt, and the policeman's superior officers would have been very glad to know that.

Gebhardt walked slowly, leaning heavily on his cane. The meeting with the policeman never failed to amuse him, and he smiled to himself at the stupidity of the English. Gebhardt looked into the jewelry shop window.

There was no expression on his face as he looked from the clocks that said six to the watches that said three. He had passed the shop faithfully every day for two weeks, but had never gone in. Gebhardt set his wrist watch and pushed open the door.

A salesman was talking with the jeweler at the far end of the counter, but they turned as the door shut. The jeweler walked toward Gebhardt and stared at him. "Yes?" asked the little man.

"My watch," said Gebhardt. "It seems to have stopped. An hour or so ago." He took off his watch and laid it on the counter.

The watch's hands indicated nine o'clock. "I see," said the jeweler. "Stopped."

Gebhardt looked toward the salesman but the salesman was busy examining a catalogue. The jeweler picked up the watch.

Gebhardt said: "And you might change the strap. That one is about worn out."

He leaned against the counter and waited. Once he looked into the back room where the jeweler had taken his watch. He could see the old man, bent over a desk, examining his watch. Gebhardt lit a cigarette and waited.

It was less than five minutes when the little man came back. He held out the watch with its new strap and Gebhardt put it on. "You should be careful," said the jeweler. "That is a fine watch."

"Yes, I know," said Gebhardt casually. "And I'm sure it will work perfectly now." He paid the jeweler, and left the shop.

All the way back to his room Gebhardt was conscious

of the strap on his wrist, but he did not look at the watch even once. After all, in his business you couldn't be too careful.

Once inside the small room where he had lived since he first came to London, Gebhardt put aside all appearance of lameness and moved about the room with quick sureness, locking the door, pulling down the curtains. Finally, he lit the light over his desk, and took off his wrist watch.

Working rapidly, he removed the straps from both ends of the watch. Then with a knife he opened the ends of the straps and, finally, from one end took out a small piece of very thin paper. He spread the paper out on his desk and with a glass began to study the message, which was written in code.

The message was short and to the point. It read: "Trucks from King Charles Square will transport Regiment 55 tomorrow A.M. Act at once."

"So," said Gebhardt softly. He burned the paper in the ash-tray. For a moment he sat thinking. He previously knew that a large number of trucks in King Charles Square would be used to carry soldiers from London to the coast. And somewhere along the route trucks and soldiers would be blown to pieces with explosives.

Gebhardt drew his suitcase from under the bed and opened it on the desk. From its nest of cotton he picked up one of the bombs. It was wide and flat, quite different in form from the usual, old-fashioned type of bomb. Attached with wire to the bottom of an automobile engine the bomb was deadly when the motor heated.

He decided to take with him in a small package about fourteen of the bombs. That was about all he could take care of in two hours. He had detailed information on all the places and garages where Army trucks were stationed, and now he consulted his information on King Charles Square. By midnight all the soldiers and mechanics were gone; at two o'clock a policeman looked in to check up. Gebhardt was very much pleased with himself. Thanks to British inefficiency, he would have the place to himself between twelve o'clock and two o'clock.

Thinking of the importance of time suddenly reminded him, and he put a new strap on his watch, and then put the watch on his wrist. Then, he sat very still, looking into space, mentally checking every detail of the plan.

Gebhardt smiled. Of course! Outside the jewelry shop he had set his watch back sixty-four minutes for the signal to the jeweler. He smiled again as he now moved the minute hand of his watch exactly sixty-four minutes ahead. Never forgetting these small details made him a good secret agent and he knew it.

When the time came Gebhardt moved carefully through the darkness of the blacked-out streets.

In the alley behind King Charles Square he stopped and looked at his watch. Twelve o'clock exactly. Gebhardt smiled. The whole thing was going like clockwork. He waited another ten minutes just to be on the safe side.

Gebhardt climbed a fence, moved carefully along a narrow space between two buildings, and came out in King Charles Square. He stood a moment, counting the black forms of the trucks.

Gebhardt moved over to the nearest truck. He set down his package, took some wire and a wire-cutter from a pocket. He slid under the truck and felt along the bottom of the engine. Lying flat on his back, working in the dark, he began to wire the bomb to the exact place he wanted it.

Somebody stepped on his ankle.

Pain shot up Gebhardt's leg, and he bit his lip, not breathing. No, he thought, there can't be anyone here. There is never anyone here at this hour. I have checked it many times. But that weight kept pressing into his ankle.

"All right, mister," said a voice. "Come out of there."

The wire-cutter fell from his fingers. Hands grabbed at Gebhardt's legs, pulled. In a panic, he kicked himself loose, got up and ran wildly.

A man shouted. Someone blew a whistle. A form jumped from nowhere and knocked him to the ground. Gebhardt drove his fist into a face, twice, pulled away free, ran on. He ran into a wall, turned the wrong way. A flashlight focused on him. He turned back, but too late.

"There! Get him! . . ."

Gebhardt drew his revolver. As he ran, he heard them shout as they came closer to him.

There was the noise of rapid gun fire behind him, and something struck him in the back. No, thought Gebhardt, the plan was perfect. There was a sharp pain. He said weakly: "No." He was dead when the soldiers reached him. He lay with his one arm stretched out in front of him, his wrist watch showing the hour.

"Imagine the nerve of that guy!" said a young soldier. "He walked in here as though we didn't even exist. That's a nice watch he has on. But it broke when he fell."

"It's an hour fast," said a second soldier. "How did that happen?"

The little jeweler was even more surprised when he read the newspaper report the next day about Gebhardt's death. I can't understand it, he thought. "The man must have been careless. Nothing went wrong on my part.

Why, I even set his watch correctly before I gave it back to him."

Exercises for Conversation

A—Answer these Questions:

1. In what city does this story take place? 2. Why does the jeweler's shop window have narrow pieces of paper pasted across it? 3. As the story opens what is the jeweler doing? 4. Why did the jeweler set the watches in his window all at three o'clock and the clocks all at six o'clock? 5. Who, after seeing this signal, entered the jeweler's shop? 6. What conversation now passed between Gebhardt and the jeweler? 7. In what part of Gebhardt's watch did the jeweler place the secret message? 8. What message was written on the thin paper placed in the strap of Gebhardt's watch? 9. What did Gebhardt take from the suitcase under his bed? 10. Were the bombs which he planned to use of normal size or were they of a special form? 11. Where did he plan to place these bombs? 12. According to his information, at what hour would he be free to work without interruption in King Charles Square? 13. Why was he very careful to set his watch exactly sixty four minutes ahead? 14. What happened that night while Gebhardt was busy beneath one of the trucks, wiring a bomb to the motor? 15. What serious error had Gebhardt made in his otherwise careful planning?

B—Give Sentences with the Following:

to pay attention to
to get out of
to lean on (against)
to *set* a watch
to pick up
to *light* a cigarette
after all
to pull down
to take out
to spread out
at once
to take care of

C—Vocabulary Practice. Answer the following correctly:

1. If you wish to have your watch repaired, you go to a (dentist, grocer, druggist, jeweler).
2. The opposite of *tall* is (low, small, short, thin).
3. What is the noun form of the adjective *stupid?* Of the adjective *lame?*
4. What is the adverb form of these adjectives; stupid, faithful, careful, perfect?
5. Which of these is a part of the body (lock, message, wrist, coast)?
6. A wrist watch is generally held to the wrist by means of a (hand, strap, lock, curtain).
7. In a shop or store, the clerk generally stands behind a (window, counter, station, catalogue).
8. Which of these has a sharp edge (motor, bomb, lamp, knife)?
9. Which of the following rhymes with the word *code* (food, coat, rod, sewed)?
10. What are the opposites of the following: wide, careful, bottom, correct?
11. What are the past tense forms of these verbs: to lie, to say, to blow, to shout, to draw, to run?
12. Only one of the above verbs is regular in form. Which is it?

ART FOR HEART'S SAKE

Rube Goldberg

Art for Heart's Sake

Rube Goldberg

PART I

"Here, take your pineapple juice," gently persuaded Koppel, the male nurse.

"No!" said Collis P. Ellsworth firmly.

"But it's good for you, sir."

"No!"

"It's the doctor's orders."

"No!"

Koppel heard the front door bell and was glad to leave the room. He found Doctor Caswell in the hall downstairs. "I can't do a thing with him," he told the doctor. "He won't take his pineapple juice. He doesn't want me to read to him. He hates the radio. He doesn't like anything."

Doctor Caswell received the information with his usual professional calm. He had done some thinking since his last visit. This was no ordinary case. The old gentleman was in pretty good shape for a man of seventy-six years. But he had to be prevented from buying things. He had suffered his last heart attack after his disastrous purchase of that small railroad out in Iowa. The attack before that came from the excitement caused by the failure of the chain of grocery stores which he had previously bought at a very high price. All of his purchases of recent years had to be liquidated at a great sacrifice both to his health and his pocketbook. Though he was still very wealthy, his health had begun to show serious effects from these various business operations.

Collis P. Ellsworth sat in a huge armchair by the window. He looked around as Doctor Caswell asked, "Well, how's the young man today?"

"Umph!" said the figure in the chair in a rather disagreeable tone.

"I hear that you haven't been obeying orders," the doctor said.

"Who's giving me orders at my time of life?"

The doctor drew up a chair and sat down close to the old man. "I've got a suggestion for you," he said quietly.

Old Ellsworth looked suspiciously over his eyeglasses. "What is it, more medicine, more automobile rides, more foolishness to keep me away from my office?"

"How would you like to take up art?" The doctor had his stethoscope ready in case the suddenness of the suggestion proved too much for the patient's heart.

But the old man's answer was a strong "Foolishness!"

"I don't mean seriously," said the doctor, relieved that nothing had happened. "Just play around with chalk and crayons. It'll be fun."

"Foolishness!"

"All right." The doctor stood up. "I just suggested it, that's all."

Collis P. paused a moment. The wrinkles in his forehead deepened a little. "Where'd you get this crazy idea, anyway?"

"Well, it's only a suggestion—"

"But, Caswell, how do I start playing with the chalk—that is, if I'm foolish enough to start?"

"I've thought of that, too. I can get a student from one of the art schools to come here once a week and show you. If you don't like it after a while, you can throw him out."

Doctor Caswell went to his friend, Judson Livingston, head of the Atlantic Art Institute, and explained the situation. Livingston had just the young man—Frank Swain, eighteen years old and an excellent student. He needed the money. He ran an elevator at night to pay for his schooling. How much would he get? Five dollars a visit. Fine.

The next afternoon young Swain was shown into the big living room. Collis P. Ellsworth looked at him suspiciously.

"Sir, I'm not an artist yet," answered the young man.

"Umph!"

Swain arranged some paper and crayons on the table. "Let's try and draw that vase over there on the table," he suggested.

"What for? It's only a bowl with some blue stains on it. Or are they green?"

"Try it, Mr. Ellsworth, please."

"Umph!" The old man took a piece of crayon in a shaky hand and drew several lines. He drew several more and then connected these crudely. "There it is, young man," he said with a tone of satisfaction. "Such foolishness!" Frank Swain was patient. He needed the five dollars. "If you want to draw you will have to look at what you're drawing, sir."

Ellsworth looked. "Gosh, it's rather pretty. I never noticed it before."

Koppel came in with the announcement that his patient had done enough for the first lesson.

"Oh, it's pineapple juice again," Ellsworth said. Swain left.

PART II

When the art student came the following week there was a drawing on the table that had a slight resemblance to a vase. The wrinkles deepened at the corners of the old gentleman's eyes as he asked, "Well, what do you think of it?"

"Not bad, sir," answered Swain. "But it's not quite straight."

"Gosh," old Ellsworth smiled, "I see. The halves don't match." He added a few lines with a shaking hand and colored the open spaces blue like a child playing with a picture book. Then he looked towards the door. "'Listen, young man," he whispered, "I want to ask you something before old pineapple juice comes back."

"Yes, sir," answered Swain politely.

"I was thinking—do you have the time to come twice a week or perhaps three times?"

"Sure, Mr. Ellsworth."

"Good. Let's make it Monday, Wednesday and Friday. Four o'clock."

Koppel entered and was greatly surprised when his patient took his pineapple juice without protest.

As the weeks went by Swain's visits grew more frequent. He brought the old man a box of water colors and some tubes of oils.

When Doctor Caswell called, Ellsworth would talk about the graceful lines of the chimney. He would mention something about the rich variety of color in a bowl of fruit. He proudly showed the various stains of paint on his dressing-gown. He would not allow his servant to send it to the cleaner's. He wanted to show the doctor how hard he'd been working.

The treatment was working perfectly. No more trips downtown to his office for the purpose of buying some business that was to fail later. No more crazy financial plans to try the strength of his tired old heart. Art was a complete cure for him.

The doctor thought it safe to allow Ellsworth to visit the Metropolitan Museum, the Museum of Modern Art and other exhibitions with Swain. An entirely new world opened up its mysteries to him. The old man showed a tremendous curiosity in the art galleries and in the painters who exhibited in them. How were the galleries run? Who selected the pictures for the exhibitions? An idea was forming in his brain.

When the late spring began to cover the fields and gardens with color Ellsworth painted a simply horrible picture which he called, "Trees Dressed in White." Then he made a surprising announcement. He was going to exhibit the picture in the summer show at the Lathrop Gallery.

For the summer show at the Lathrop Gallery was the biggest art exhibition of the year—in quality, if not in size. The life-time dream of every important artist in the United States was a prize from this exhibition. Among the paintings of this distinguished group of artists Ellsworth was now going to place his "Trees Dressed in White," which resembled a handful of salad-dressing thrown violently against the side of a house.

"If the newspapers hear about this, everyone in town will be laughing at Mr. Ellsworth. We've got to stop him," said Koppel.

"No," warned the doctor. "We can't interfere with

him now and take a chance of ruining all the good work which we have done."

To the complete surprise of all three—and especially Swain—"Trees Dressed in White" was accepted for the Lathrop show. Not only was Mr. Ellsworth crazy, thought Koppel, but the Lathrop Gallery was crazy, too.

Fortunately the painting was hung in an inconspicuous place where it did not draw any special notice or comment. Young Swain slipped into the museum one afternoon and blushed to the top of his ears when he saw "Trees Dressed in White," a loud, ugly picture on a wall otherwise covered with paintings of beauty and harmony. As two laughing students stopped before the strange picture Swain left hurriedly. He could not bear to hear what they had to say.

During the course of the exhibition the old man kept on taking lessons, seldom mentioning his picture in the exhibition. He was unusually cheerful. Every time Swain entered the room he found Ellsworth laughing to himself. Maybe Koppel was right. The old man was crazy. But it seemed equally strange that the Lathrop committee should encourage his craziness by accepting his picture.

Two days before the close of the exhibition a special messenger brought a long official-looking envelope to Mr. Ellsworth while Swain, Koppel and the doctor were in the room. "Read it to me," said the old man. "My eyes are tired from painting."

> "It gives the Lathrop Gallery great pleasure to announce that the First Prize of $1,000 has been awarded to Collis P. Ellsworth for his painting, "Trees Dressed in White."

Swain and Koppel were so surprised that they could not say a word. Doctor Caswell, exercising his professional self-control with a supreme effort, said, "Congratulations,

Mr. Ellsworth. Fine, fine. . . . See, see. . . . Of course, I didn't expect such great news. But, but—well, now, you'll have to admit that art is much more satisfying than business."

"Art has nothing to do with it," said the old man sharply. "I bought the Lathrop Gallery last month."

Exercises for Conversation

A–Answer the Following:

1. Identify the following characters of this story: Koppel, Swain, Ellsworth. 2. Why was Ellsworth under the care of a doctor? 3. Was Ellsworth a very wealthy or a very poor man? 4. Had his recent business operations been very successful or very unsuccessful? 5. How had these business operations affected his health? 6. Why did Dr. Caswell suggest that Mr. Ellsworth take up art? 7. Whom did Dr. Caswell obtain to give lessons to Mr. Ellsworth? 8. Did Mr. Ellsworth's interest in art grow or lessen? 9. Did he decide to increase or decrease his lessons with young Swain? 10. Instead of going to his office, where did Mr. Ellsworth now begin to go with Swain? 11. Why did Mr. Ellsworth show a particular interest in how the various art galleries were run and in how the pictures were selected for exhibition? 12. Did Mr. Ellsworth choose a well-known or a little known gallery in which to exhibit his picture "Trees Dressed in White"? 13. Was the picture deserving of the prize it won later or did it look like a "handful of salad-dressing thrown violently" against a wall? 14. What message did a special messenger bring one day in an official-looking envelope to Mr. Ellsworth? 15. By what means had Mr. Ellsworth assured himself of winning this prize?

B–Give Sentences with the Following:

to be in good shape
to keep away from
in case
in case of
to play around with
to *run* an elevator

to show someone in (out)
to go by
to hear about
to have (got) to
to take a chance
to keep on doing something
to have nothing (something) to do with

C—Vocabulary Practice. Answer each of the following correctly:

1. A common synonym for *wealthy* is (well, healthy, poor, rich).
2. Using the correct prefix in each case, give the opposites of the following: agreeable, correct, patient, satisfied.
3. Which of the following is used to hold flowers (vase, space, artist, envelope)?
4. Which of the following is a synonym for *crazy* (bright, important, insane, horrible)?
5. Which of these is the opposite of *ugly* (loud, intelligent, beautiful, strange)?
6. A person blushes when he is (tired, hungry, distinguished, embarrassed).
7. What is the noun form of the adjective *crazy?* Of the adjective *insane?*
8. Which of these is the opposite of *sad* (official, satisfying, cheerful, violent)?
9. If I cannot *stand* something, I cannot (hear it, bear it, find it, draw it).
10. To *keep on* doing something is to (stop doing it, continue doing it, begin doing it).
11. What is the full form of the following contractions (he'd, I'm, you're, I'll, she's)?
12. With which of the following does the word *bear* rhyme (near, rear, pear, fear)?

ALL ABOARD

Walter Davenport

All Aboard

Walter Davenport

PART I

Ordinary men like you and me would have told young Hillegas the facts at the beginning, using no more words than would be necessary for simple courtesy.

But that wasn't Ham's way.

I have heard it said that Ham Mason should have been a dramatist or a public speaker because he loved to talk so much. However, the Mason House, of which Ham was proprietor, clerk and general repair man, was obvious proof that he was no hotel man worth mentioning.

"Glad to take care of you, mister," said Ham to the young fellow who had arrived on the noon train with the most expensive traveling-bag the Mason House had ever held.

"Let me see." Ham looked at the board where, in great disorder, hung the keys to the various rooms.

"Four, five, six, sev—I can let you have number six, mister—mister." Ham turned the register around in order to see the name of the new guest—Mr. Hillegas. "I can put you in number six, Mr. Hillegas, but I'm sorry I can't give you no bath. There's a nice bath just down the hall a little ways."

And Ham took the young fellow's important looking bag and led the way up the stairs, talking constantly all the way about how he was very busy teaching a new maid her duties because Jennie Burkett, the regular maid, was home looking after her father, who had been struck by a streetcar on Saturday night, and how number eight was the only room with a private bath and that Clyde Betts, his brother-in-law who traveled for Gibson's wholesale groceries, always had to have number eight and that Clyde was due on his monthly call at Milestown that afternoon.

Mr. Hillegas did not seem interested, yet he didn't show any irritation. An older man would have tried to silence Ham in one way or another. Ham always took advantage of a young audience, knowing its durability.

"From New York, you say," said Ham, showing Hillegas into room number six and setting down the impressive bag. "What's your business?"

"Investments," said the young fellow, "I'm with Crissman and Maginley, one of the oldest investment houses in New York. I haven't been with them long. I've come to see Mr. Edward Colesberry. Do you know him?"

True genius can make use of any opportunity, and here Ham saw a real chance to exhibit his gifts of eloquence.

"Ed Colesberry?" he cried. "Why, Mr. Hillegas, if Ed Colesberry and me were blood brothers, I couldn't have known him no better. So you came all the way out here from New York to see Ed Colesberry, hey?"

Ham was very much pleased with himself.

"Mr. Colesberry and a few others," said the young man. "You see, I haven't been with the firm long. Mr. Colesberry used to do business with us, and they decided to send some of us younger men out to look up old customers who haven't been buying for a long while."

"Well, Mr. Hillegas," said Ham, "I don't plan to take up your good time, but maybe you'd like to get an idea about the kind of a fellow you came out to see."

Hillegas said that he would be glad to learn something about Ed Coleberry, and he gave Ham a large cigar.

"Ed was sixty years old last month," said Ham. "Getting along in years. He and I went to school together, so what I'm telling you is so. Most popular boy in the county, Ed Colesberry. The most intelligent too. Half the business men in town wanted him to work for them when he graduated from high school.

" 'Ham,' he says to me, 'I'm going to work for Willis Deemer for a while. Then as soon as I get a little money together, I'm going to New York where a fellow has a chance to do big things. I'm not going to bury myself here in Milestown. I'm not going to be happy until I hear the conductor on the New York train say, "All aboard for New York City!" '

"Well, Ed worked in Willis Deemer's hardware store for a year and did so well that Willis, who was getting along in years, offered to make him a partner. Ed was refusing for the fourth time, saying that he didn't want to be tied down, when Willis died and Willis' widow begged Ed to take over the business for a while because it was all that Willis had left to her and the children.

"Ed said all right, that he'd stay a little longer, and in a few months the Deemer hardware store was the biggest in the county and getting bigger, and Ed was in love with Maureen Brent, whose father was our biggest real estate man.

" 'I'm only staying a while longer,' Ed told me, 'and then Maureen and I are getting married and moving to New York where we can get somewheres. I'll be smiling when the conductor on that train yells, "All aboard." '

PART II

"Well, Mr. Hillegas, Maureen got sick, and the wedding had to be postponed a couple of times, and when they did get married the doctor said that it would not be good for her to move so close to the ocean as New York, for a year or so anyway.

"So Ed stayed in Milestown, making Willis Deemer's widow rich and at the same time becoming a partner in the business so that it would be easier for him to carry it on. Of course, at the same time, he was making money himself too.

" 'But as soon as Maureen can go east,' said Ed, 'we're going to New York. We're not going to bury ourselves in Milestown.'

"Ed was a really ambitious fellow, Mr. Hillegas. Do you understand?"

"Yes," said young Hillegas. "And he was determined to go to New York, in a way."

"That's it exactly," said Ham. "And about a couple of years after the time I was just telling you about her father started that real estate development over on Gobbler's Hill, calling it Mount Airy, and though Ed objected strongly, saying that he didn't want to get tied down because he and Maureen were surely going to New York as soon as their new baby was able to travel, they made him one of the big men in the business, since they thought that this was the best way to make it a definite success.

"Of course, you're wondering wny Milestown didn't tell Ed to go on to New York if he didn't like it here, but you have to remember, Mr. Hillegas, that Ed was one of those fellows who can get away with that sort of thing, and besides Milestown just didn't want to lose Ed, because everything he got into, no matter if he wanted to or not, went big, and people trusted him.

"For instance, the real estate development in which everybody had invested their good money was doing just fine when Ketchum Brent, Maureen's father, died, and Ed simply had to take over Ketchum's work. Besides, all Ketchum's money was in the development, and, now that it came to Maureen, Ed just had to devote his time to it. I don't think Milestown has ever had a bigger money maker than that development, Mr. Hillegas. But Ed was as angry as a bear.

"Yes, sir," said Ham. "And it was very strange the way that things happened. The development was a big success, and Maureen had her second baby, and Ed made an arrangement with the bank to take care of his and Maureen's real estate holdings. He sold out his half of the hardware business at a big profit and was looking for someone to buy his house.

" 'Ham,' he said to me, 'I'm going to New York. Yes, sir, the time has come and I'm a young man yet. Maureen's not any too well, and she needs care by special doctors, and the kids will have special schools, and it's only a matter of days now when I'll hear the conductor of the New York train yelling, "All aboard!" Yes, sir.'

"And, Mr. Hillegas, just at that time the savings-bank almost failed completely. Yes, sir. Tom Staub, the cashier, left town one night with almost all the money, and it looked as though most of the working people in Milestown had lost all their money.

"It certainly looked for a while as if the savings bank would have to close, and while the poor people would like to have killed Tom Staub they were thinking more about saving the bank in some way, and they just naturally began insisting that Ed Colesberry do something.

"Maureen, who by this time also wanted to go to New York, just made Ed take over the bank. Ed never had any banking experience, but he didn't need any as far as I could see. He just took over, and the bank did what everything else did—just what Ed wanted it to do. It took a little time but Ed saved it.

"He came out of it president of the bank. It's the biggest savings bank in this end of the state today. But when Ed took over the bank he came to me and said that no matter what happened he was going to New York and nobody could stop him. I couldn't help laughing a little."

Ham paused impressively.

"So I'll find him at the savings bank, hey?" said young Hillegas.

"No," said Ham, "you won't, Mr. Hillegas. Ed's gone to New York. I was coming to that. Ed died last week. Stroke. In his will which he made right after they made him head of the bank he gave a million dollars to Milestown and the rest to Maureen and the children—provided that they buried him in New York. He was determined to get there somehow."

Exercises for Conversation

PART I

A—Answer these Questions:

1. Why did some people say that Ham Mason should have been a dramatist or a public speaker? 2. What was the name of the hotel of which Ham was proprietor, clerk, and general repair man? 3. Did the general appearance of the hotel indicate that Ham was a good hotel man or a poor one? 4. Who

was the visitor who arrived at the Mason House at the time of this story? 5. Why had Mr. Hillegas come to this town? 6. Why was Mr. Mason unable to give Mr. Hillegas a room with bath? 7. What does the author mean when he says that Ham always took advantage of a young audience, knowing its durability? 8. Did Ham Mason claim that he knew Ed Colesberry well or only distantly? 9. Was Ed Colesberry, according to Ham, a capable person or a man of little ability? 10. What was the main ambition of Ed Colesberry's life? 11. Why did Ed Colesberry not wish to remain in Milestown? 12. In what kind of store did he first begin to work? 13. What are some of the things which one buys in a hardware store? 14. What were the circumstances which finally forced Ed to take over Deemer's Hardware Store?

B—Give Sentences with the Following:

a little ways
to lead the way
to look after
to be due
to take advantage of
to make use of
to do business with
to look up
for a while
to get along in years
as soon as
to take over

PART II

A—Answer these Questions:

1. Under Ed Colesberry's management did Deemer's Hardware Store do well or poorly? 2. What did Maureen's illness prevent her and Ed from doing? 3. Why didn't Ed wish to take part at first in the real estate development started by Maureen's father? 4. What is a "real estate development" and what is its purpose? 5. Was the real estate development a success or a failure? 6. Why did Ed finally make an arrangement with the bank to take care of his real estate and why did he sell his half of the hardware business? 7. Why did the savings bank of the town almost fail at this time? 8. Why did the poor people who had all of their money in the bank insist that Ed Colesberry take it over? 9. Had Ed had much or little

banking experience previously? 10. Did the bank finally fail or did Ed save it? 11. Of what did Ed Colesberry die? 12. What were the terms of Ed Colesberry's will when he died?

B—Give Sentences with the Following:

to get sick
to get married
to wonder why
to get away with
to take care of
to sell out
to look for
to be a matter of
to leave town
as though
no matter what
provided that

C—Vocabulary Practice. Answer the following correctly:

1. A common synonym for the word *courteous* is (rough, distant, bold, polite).

2. What is the noun form of the adjective *courteous;* of the word *polite?*

3. A dramatist writes (novels, plays, essays, poetry).

4. What do we call a man who writes novels? A man who writes poetry?

5. In a hotel one generally has to sign a (bill, register, check, document).

6. What is the adverb form of the word *obvious?*

7. A common synonym for the word *corridor* is (entrance, bath, roof, hall).

8. The opposite of *wholesale* is (delayed, ready, in large quantities, retail).

9. What is the past tense form of these verbs: to set, to sit, to make, to decide, to buy, to graduate, to beg, to leave, to refuse?

10. Which of the above-mentioned verbs are regular in form and which are irregular?

11. To which of the following would you go to buy a hammer (drug-store, grocery store, hardware store, filling station)?

12. To *put off* something is to (repeat it, need it, put it away, postpone it).

13. The opposite of *ambitious* is (tired, energetic, lazy, bright).

14. In what two ways can the word *close* be pronounced? What two different meanings does the word *close* have when given these different pronunciations?

WILL OF THE WIND

William Brandon

Will of the Wind

William Brandon

Mrs. Hackett found her in her bedroom crying. She stood in the doorway and said seriously: "I came in to borrow some sugar, Sylvia. The door was open so I just walked in. Now what on earth's wrong with you?"

Sylvia sat up and dried her eyes. Her skirt was wrinkled and her black hair hung in disorder over her forehead. A pin had come out of her imitation lace collar and it had fallen down to catch in the little red buckle at her waist. She said shakily, "Hello, Mrs. Hackett. Nothing."

Mrs. Hackett drew down the corners of her mouth. "Nothing, indeed. It's because of Chip wanting to leave here and go to Canton. Isn't it? Of course it is."

Sylvia pushed her hair aside out of her eyes. "I won't do it," she said angrily. "I won't."

"Mm," Mrs. Hackett said sourly. " 'A boy's will is the wind's will.' That's a poem. It's the truest thing in the world. It doesn't do any good to fight against it. Remember that and you'll have it easier."

"I won't do it. I won't move around to one mill after another all my life, and never have anything, no home, and no—no nothing! I won't!"

"Well, it's his job if he wants to give it up."

"It isn't! It's just as much mine as it is his. I don't believe in that old idea that a woman's just a—a slave, to follow a man around whatever he happens to want to do!"

"Oh, you don't," Mrs. Hackett said. "And just what can you do about it?"

Sylvia bowed her head and dried her cheeks with her handkerchief. "I don't know," she said.

"Of course you don't. You're nothing but a child," Mrs. Hackett said. "You'll be twenty years finding out what to do and by that time it'll be too late to do you any good. Unless there's somebody around to tell you to begin with. Somebody who knows."

Sylvia was not impressed. "What could you tell me, Mrs. Hackett? What could anyone do? I've argued with him until I'm almost crazy but he—he doesn't even listen any more. He's got his mind set on moving on, to something different that won't be any different at all, and then he'll want to go again, and—"

" 'A boy's will is the wind's will,' " said Mrs. Hackett. "That's what the poem says. It's just as true of a man or an old man, for that matter. The older they get the truer it gets, I guess. Only they rather give up trying to do anything about it after so long a time." She pushed up her lower lip and looked down her nose at Sylvia. "Like Mr. Hackett."

Sylvia looked up, surprised. "You mean Mr. Hackett used to—want to—"

"He was the hardest man to hold down in this town. He got tired of everything, that was his trouble. It's a sort of laziness, that's all it is. But he stuck here. He stuck, all right."

"Why?" Sylvia asked. "What did you do?"

"Well," Mrs. Hackett said, "you can take it for what it's worth, Sylvia. It worked with Mr. Hackett, I know that."

"But what was it?"

"Whenever he got all excited about leaving here and going away some place to look for something he thought was better, I simply gave him his way. I didn't oppose him in the least."

Sylvia looked disappointed and confused. "Oh."

"But," Mrs. Hackett said profoundly, "he didn't know it. I always took him on a trip. Just a week or so. And I kept him on the jump every minute of it. I always liked little trips around, anyway. Well, by the time that man would get home again he'd be so tired of jumping around that he wouldn't have left for a thousand dollars. That," Mrs. Hackett said, "is something you find out about men, Sylvia. They like to start but they like to get back home a whole lot more."

Sylvia said doubtfully. "It doesn't seem that Chip would—"

"Maybe he wouldn't. I'm the last person in the world to try to give other people advice, Sylvia. Nobody wants it and I guess everyone has to live his own life, anyway. But Mr. Hackett says that they're shutting down the mill for a week, and if Chip was to spend that week in a car traveling along fast from one place to another, without even a chance to catch his breath . . . Well, 'a boy's will is the wind's will,' the idea of that is that the wind can change in a minute."

"But what if he wouldn't want to go?"

"Mm. You tell him you want a little vacation before you move to Canton. If he thinks that you've given in to him about moving to Canton, he'll take you. You try it and see."

They went up into Michigan, west to Wisconsin, down through Minnesota and Iowa and St. Louis to Memphis, east to Knoxville and up through Louisville to come home. They were gone six days. Each day Sylvia arranged it so that they got up very early and were on the highway by daylight and she kept on the job, planning the things to visit at the next stop, until late at night. She called upon Chip to stop often at roadside stands and she filled him with hot dogs, soft drinks and bad coffee. She was surprised and delighted at the dull look that appeared in his eyes on the third day.

Mrs. Hackett came over the day after they returned to bring back the cup of sugar she had borrowed. She said, "Well!" and paused expectantly, holding the cup of sugar in both hands.

"He went back to work today," Sylvia said. There was a tired note in her voice. "He hasn't said a thing about going to Canton for several days."

"Mm! And what did he say when he got home?" She asked. "That he never thought home would look so good to him?"

Sylvia nodded. She sat down on a kitchen chair and for a moment seemed lost in thought. "He said exactly that," she said at last.

"You won't even be able to get him to move out of the house to go to a movie for a month. I told you. Wind's will, that's the poem. They're all alike, all men." She put the cup of sugar on the kitchen cabinet and looked at Sylvia. "But I wouldn't say that you look so happy about it, Sylvia. But you're tired."

Sylvia rested her chin on her hand. She sighed and said, "I'm a little tired of this town, I guess. I was just thinking, when we came back yesterday, and it looked so . . . so old and so dirty and dull and tiresome . . . and

I thought that we'll spend all our lives here, with nothing to do except the same old . . . oh, I was just thinking."

Mrs. Hackett drew back and looked at Sylvia seriously and then said. "You're just tired, Sylvia. My goodness, that long trip—"

Sylvia looked up and her eyes were shining. "But I'm not tired," she said. "I had a wonderful time."

Exercises for Conversation

A—Answer the Following:

1. What is the significance of the title of this story, "Will of the Wind"? 2. Is the wind something which changes with great or little frequency? 3. In this story who, besides Chip, the husband, also changed rather suddenly in attitude and idea? 4. Where does this story take place? 5. As the story opens, why is Sylvia crying? 6. What does Mrs. Hackett come to borrow? 7. What had Mrs. Hackett always done when Mr. Hackett got all excited about leaving and moving to another town to work? 8. What did Mrs. Hackett suggest that Sylvia and her husband do during the week in which the mill was to shut down? 9. What trip did Sylvia and her husband finally take during this week? 10. Did they travel much or little during this trip? 11. What was Sylvia's purpose in filling her husband with hot dogs, soft drinks and bad coffee? 12. Was her husband apparently very happy or very sad to get back home? 13. Did he talk much or little now about moving to Canton? 14. What was Sylvia's reaction when they got back to their home town again? 15. To what extent had Sylvia enjoyed the trip?

B—Give Sentences with the Following:

to be wrong with
to give something up
to have one's mind set on
at all
for that matter
the older, the truer (the sooner, the better, etc.)

used to
to give someone his way
to catch one's breath
to give in to
to have a good time

C—Vocabulary Practice. Answer each of the following correctly:

1. Which of these is a part of the face (hair, collar, forehead, waist)?
2. Every belt usually has a (sleeve, buckle, handkerchief, chance).
3. A man of strong *will* is a man of (good education, determination, imagination, physical strength).
4. What are the past tense forms of these verbs: to stick, to argue, to hold, to bow, to nod, to keep, to catch, to shut?
5. Which of these is a common synonym for *shut* (open, begin, admire, close)?
6. *Hot dogs* are also often called (soft-drinks, roadside-stands, friendly enemies, frankfurters).
7. Along which of these can you drive in your car (kitchen-cabinet, post-office, highway, hot dog-stand)?
8. What is the difference in use between the two words *advice* and *advise?*
9. What is the noun form of the adjective *lazy?* Of the adjective *frequent?*
10. What are the opposites of these words: true, lower, hard, lazy, borrow, lost, dirty?
11. Which of these has a sharp point at one end (slave, mill, soft-drink, pin)?

IRENE'S SISTER

Vina Delmar

Irene's Sister

Vina Delmar

This is a story of 19—, the year that the schools did not open on time, the year that plague descended and caught us as terrified and as defenseless as though we were inhabitants in some medieval city faced with a new and terrible sickness.

I was a child at that time. My friends and I did not understand. We asked questions but the grown-ups were as confused and as frightened as ourselves. "It's infantile paralysis," they told us. "It kills you or else it leaves you crippled forever. Don't go too close to anybody and don't touch anything that a strange child has handled."

Fear held us so completely that we forgot how to laugh or to play. I can remember lying in bed at night waiting for the disease to strike at me. I had no idea what form it might take and I lay very quietly praying that when next I wished to move my legs or arms I would be able to do so as I had always done in the past.

There was one among us, however, who had no fear of the terrible plague. That girl was Irene Crane. In my mind's eye I can still see her as she was back there in those difficult days. She was a yellow-haired child with a happy ring to her laughter and the greatest capacity for fun of anyone I've ever known. She was the school beauty, popular with teachers and pupils alike and if she was not the most intelligent of our group that was easily forgiven for one does not expect to find genius in a flower.

Irene had a sister who was a year younger. Her mother called her Caroline, but outside the house she was known simply as Irene's sister. It was natural for her to be Irene's sister just as it was natural for us to be a nameless group of girls known as Irene's friends. Irene was the center of our small world and we revolved about her brilliance and asked for no recognition for ourselves. Irene's sister, conscious of her inability to compete with the beauty and enchanting manner of Irene, was perfectly content to be only a pale reflection of our yellow-haired commander.

Only once were we unable to think with Irene. That was when she said: "I'm not scared of that infantile paralysis. We won't get it. You'll see. None of us will."

We were ashamed of our fears but there they were just the same.

I can remember the day that we all went over to Ginny Smith's house for games and light refreshments. For our health's sake, the grown-ups looked upon the party with some doubts, but for the good of our morale they consented.

"After all," they said to one another, "it's the same group of girls who see each other almost every day anyway. It'll be all right."

"It's the same group except for Irene's sister." She hadn't been invited because she was not in our grade at school and Ginny Smith hadn't known that Irene had a sister.

"It doesn't matter," Irene said. "Caroline isn't feeling well. She has an upset stomach, I guess."

The games were fun, the food was wonderful, we thought. It had been a beautiful day in which we all seemed to forget for a while that something strange and terrible walked everywhere about us beyond the pleasant comfort of Ginny Smith's house. We were just collecting our hats and coats, ready to leave, and thanking Ginny for a lovely day when the phone rang.

I can still see Ginny Smith's mother as she stood talking on that phone. I can see the look of horror that appeared upon her face. I can still see the tears that were in her eyes when she hung up the receiver and turned to face us.

"Irene," she said in a choked voice, "that was your mother. Your sister has infantile paralysis. You can't go home. You'll have to stay here." There was a horrible pause. Then, "It's too late for us to be afraid of you, child. You've been here all day."

We went away without touching Irene, some of us without speaking to her. The plague had reached out and struck at us. We hurried home afraid of each other, ashamed of our fear and unable to keep back the thought that tomorrow we would all be attacked by death or lameness.

Irene stayed with the Smiths, I suppose. I don't know. I hurried home and wrote at once to my father. It must have been an emotional, crazy little letter in which I begged him to come and get me and take me to safety somewhere, anywhere. I did not know that the plague was widespread. I thought it was just in our town. Anyway my father came and took me away. I went happily, thankfully, but I did not know as I went that it would be fifteen years before I ever saw that town again.

I was a woman when I returned to visit and the first night I was back I was surprised to find that my hostess's living room was decorated as though for a party.

"Just the old group," she explained, "and their husbands. You remember Ginny Smith, Lila Day, the Crane girls and that group."

A strange feeling of terror ran through me at the mention of the Crane girls. I was a child again frightened before a terrible mysterious force that wanted to kill me.

"I remember them all," I said. "How are the Crane girls?"

"The same as ever, just exactly the same. One popular and one a complete failure."

"It's cruel to say that," I protested. "Caroline had paralysis. How can you expect her to be—"

"But it's Irene who's the failure. She's silly. Remember how she used to laugh and play jokes all the time? She's still the same, but now everything she says sounds a little silly. But you can't invite Caroline without inviting Irene so we—"

"But is Caroline well?"

"Of course she is. She had good care and good sense used on her and she's as fine as anyone. A lot finer, I guess. She went through so much pain and suffering that she has more depth and understanding than most people. She's so strong and dependable. Of course she thanks her doctor and her nurse and her mother for everything and they say that it was Caroline's patience and courage that helped them to help her. Wait till you see her. She's—"

It was at that moment that the doorbell rang and that my hostess's mother, who was looking out of an upstairs window, called to us. I'll never forget her words. She called, "Daughter, go to the door. It's Caroline's sister."

My hostess looked at me and laughed. "What did I tell you?" she said.

Exercises for Conversation

A—Answer the Following:

1. Of what "plague" is the author speaking in this story? 2. Is this story written in the first person, the second person, or the third person? 3. Why was Irene Crane so popular as a child? 4. Why was Irene's sister Caroline always referred to, outside her home, simply as Irene's sister? 5. Was Irene's sister jealous of Irene's popularity or was she content to be only a "pale reflection" of her more popular sister? 6. Why did the grown-ups look with some doubts upon the party at Ginny Smith's house? 7. Why hadn't Irene's sister been invited to this party? 8. Just as the girls were leaving the party, what sad message did Mrs. Smith receive by phone? 9. Why did the author write to her father asking him to take her away from this town? 10. When, finally, did she return to this town? 11. What changes had occurred in the Crane girls in the meantime? 12. Which of the Crane girls was now popular, which a failure?

B—Give Sentences with the Following:

on time
at night
in the past
to be known as
to be ashamed of
for the good of
after all
not to matter
for a while
to hang up
to play jokes on
all day

C—Vocabulary Practice. Answer each of the following correctly:

1. The word *terrified* means (amused, pleased, surprised, frightened).

2. *Grown-ups* are (children, youngsters, adults, parents).

3. Which *two* of the following may be used as the past tense form of the verb *to lie,* depending upon its meaning (laid, lied, lain, lay, led)?

4. If a person is yellow-haired, we generally refer to him or to her as a (brunette, redhead, blonde, fool).

5. What is the noun form of the verb *to laugh?* What is the noun form of the adjective *popular?*

6. Which of these is a synonym for the word *enchanting* (ugly, healthy, scared, charming)?

7. Which of the following rhymes with the word *known* (town, ton, tune, tone)?

8. How many syllables does each of the following words contain: horror, appeared, phone, seemed, consented, looked?

9. *To beg* is to (protest, compete, ask, suppose).

10. What are the opposites of the words: popular, happy, late, dependable, strong, upstairs?

11. *Silly* means (foolish, fine, painful, forgiven).

12. When you finish telephoning what do you do with the receiver (pick it up, put it away, hang it up, throw it down)?

THE WRONG HOUSE

James N. Young

The Wrong House

James N. Young

The night was dark. And the house was dark. Dark—and silent. The two men ran toward it quietly. They slipped quickly through the dark bushes which surrounded the house. They reached the porch, ran quickly up the steps, kneeled down, breathing heavily, in the dark shadows. They waited—listening.

Silence. Perfect silence. Then—out of the blackness—a whisper: "We can't stay out here. . . . Take this suitcase. . . . Let me try those keys. We've got to get in!"

Ten—twenty—thirty seconds. With one of the keys the one man opened the door. Silently, the two men then entered the house, closed the door behind them, locked it.

Whispering, they discussed the situation. They wondered if they had awakened anyone in the house.

After a time: "Let's have a look at this place." "Careful, Hasty!" "Oh, there isn't anybody awake!" And the soft rays of a flashlight swept the room.

It was a large room. A living-room. Rugs, carefully rolled, lay piled on one side. The furniture—chairs, tables, couches—was covered by sheets. Dust lay like a light snow over everything.

The man who held the flashlight spoke first. "Well, Blackie," he said, "we're in luck. Looks as if the family's away."

"Yeah. Gone for the summer, I guess. We better make sure, though. Huh."

Together they searched the house. They went on tiptoe through every room. There could be no doubt about it. The family *was* away. Had been away for weeks.

Yes, Hasty Hogan and Blackie Burns were in luck. Only once in the past ten days had their luck failed them. It had been with them when they made their big robbery—their truly magnificent robbery—on the Coast. It had been with them during their thousand mile trip eastward, by automobile. It had been with them every moment—but one.

That moment had come just one hour before. It came when Blackie, driving the car, ran over a policeman. And Blackie, thinking of the suitcase at Hasty's feet, had driven away. Swiftly.

There had been a chase, of course. A wild, crazy chase. And when a bullet had punctured the gasoline tank they had had to abandon the car. But luck or no luck, here they were. Alone, and without a car, in a completely strange town. But safe and sound—with the *suitcase.*

The suitcase lay in the center of the table, in the center of the room. In the suitcase, neat little package on neat little package, lay nearly three hundred thousand dollars!

"Listen," said Mr. Hogan. "We have to get a car. Quick, too. And we can't steal one—and use it. It's too dangerous. We have to buy one. That means that we have to wait until the stores open. That will be about eight o'clock in this town."

"But what are we going to do with that?" And Mr. Burns pointed to the suitcase.

"Hide it right here. Sure! Why not? It's much safer here than with us—until we get a car."

And so they hid the suitcase. They carried it down to

the cellar. Buried it deep in some coal which lay in a corner of the cellar. After this, just before dawn, they slipped out.

"Say, Blackie," Mr. Hogan remarked as they walked down the street, "the name of the gentleman we're visiting is Mr. Samuel W. Rogers."

"How do you know?"

"Saw it on some of them books. He's surely got a wonderful library, hasn't he?"

The automobile salesrooms opened at eight o'clock, as Mr. Hogan had supposed. Shortly before nine, Mr. Hogan and Mr. Burns had a car. A very nice little car. Very quiet. Very inconspicuous. And very speedy. The dealer lent them his license plates and away they rode.

Three blocks from the house, they stopped. Mr. Hogan got out. Walked toward the house. He'd just go around to the rear, he thought, and slip in.

Fifty yards from the house he stopped. Stared, swore softly. The front door was open. The window shades were up. The family had returned!

Well, what bad luck. And what could they do? Break into the cellar that night, and pick up the suitcase? No—too dangerous. Mr. Hogan would have to think of something.

"Leave it to me, kid," he told Mr. Burns. "You drive the car. I'll do the special brain work. Let's find a telephone. Quick!"

Ten minutes later, Mr. Hogan was consulting a telephone directory. Yes, there it was—Samuel W. Rogers, Plainview 6329. A moment later he was talking to the surprised Mr. Rogers.

"Hello," he began, "is this Mr. Rogers—Mr. Samuel Rogers?"

"Yes, this is Mr. Rogers."

Mr. Hogan cleared his throat. "Mr. Rogers," he said —and his tone was sharp, official, impressive—"this is Headquarters, Police Headquarters, talking. I am Simpson. Sergeant Simpson, of the detective division—"

"Yes, yes!" came over the wire.

"The Chief—the Chief of Police, you know,"—here Mr. Hogan lowered his voice a little—"has ordered me to get in touch with you. He's sending me out with one of our men to see you."

"Am I in trouble of some kind?" asked Mr. Rogers.

"No, no, no. Nothing like that. But I have something of great importance to talk to you about."

"Very well," came the voice of Mr. Rogers. "I'll wait for you."

"And, Mr. Rogers," Mr. Hogan cautioned, "please keep quiet about this. Don't say anything to anybody. You'll understand why when I see you."

On the way back to the house Mr. Hogan explained his idea to Mr. Burns.

Within ten minutes "Sergeant Simpson" and "Detective Johnson" were conversing with the surprised Mr. Rogers. Mr. Rogers was a small man. Rather insignificant. He had pale blue eyes. Not much of a chin. A funny little face. He was nervous—a badly frightened man.

Mr. Hogan told the whole story. Somewhat changed. *Very much* changed. And Mr. Rogers was surprised, but delighted.

He accompanied Mr. Hogan to the cellar. And together they dug up the suitcase. Took it to the living-room, opened it, saw that it had not been touched—that it really did hold a small fortune. Bills, bills, bills.

Mr. Hogan closed the suitcase.

"And now, Mr. Rogers," he announced, in his best official manner, "Johnson and I must run along. The chief wants a report—quick. We have to catch the rest of the robbers. I'll keep in touch with you."

He picked up the suitcase and rose. Mr. Burns also rose. Mr. Rogers also rose. The trio walked to the door. Mr. Rogers opened it. "Come on in, boys," he said pleasantly—and in walked three men. Large men. Strong men. Men in police uniform who, without fear, stared at Mr. Hasty Hogan and Mr. Blackie Burns.

"What does *this* mean, Mr. Rogers," asked Mr. Hogan.

"It's quite simple," said Mr. Rogers. "It just happens that *I* am the Chief of Police."

Exercises for Conversation

A–Answer these Questions:

1. Where does this story take place? 2. As the story opens, what do we find the two characters, Mr. Hogan and Mr. Burns, doing? 3. Why, when they discovered that there was no one in the house, did they think that they were in luck? 4. What seemed to indicate that the family was away for the summer? 5. What was the single occasion during the previous ten days that the luck of Mr. Hogan and Mr. Burns had failed them? 6. Why did they have to abandon their car? 7. Where had they obtained the large sum of money which they carried in the suitcase? 8. Where did they finally decide to hide the suitcase? 9. Why did they decide to buy an automobile rather than to steal one? 10. Why did they choose a rather quiet, inconspicuous car? 11. When they again went back to the house, what did they discover? 12. When Mr. Hogan called Mr. Rogers by telephone, who did he say that he was? 13. To what extent did Mr. Rogers cooperate with "Sergeant Simpson" and "Detective Johnson"? 14. When Mr. Hogan and Mr. Rogers

were about to leave, what three men were waiting for them? 15. Who did Mr. Rogers happen to be?

B—Give Sentences with the Following:

to kneel down
to have (got) to
to be in luck
to make sure
to be away
to run over someone
safe and sound
shortly after
to get in touch with
to be in trouble
to keep quiet
on the way back

C—Vocabulary Practice. Answer the following correctly:

1. *To whisper* is to (yell, cry, speak loudly, speak softly).
2. Which of the following do we find on a bed (bushes, couches, sheets, tanks)?
3. If someone does something *silently,* he does it (impressively, noiselessly, quickly, well).
4. To walk *on tiptoe* is to walk (well, quickly, carelessly, quietly).
5. What is the past tense form of these verbs: to hide, to slide, to slip, to fail, to stare, to dig, to take, to run?
6. Which of the above verbs are regular in form? Which are irregular?
7. What is the past-participial form of the following verbs: to hide, to take, to run, to see?
8. When we say that the "shades were up", we are referring to which part of a house (the porch, the entrance, the cellar, the windows)?
9. What is the noun form of the verb *to fall?*
10. *Speedy* means (slow, fast, careful, careless).
11. The opposite of to *pick up something* is to (put it down, put it away, put it back, put it off).
12. With which of the following does the word *neat* rhyme (fit, feet, fate, fat)?

DETOUR TO ROMANCE

Gilbert Wright

Detour to Romance

Gilbert Wright

Located in the check-room in Union Station as I am, I see everybody that comes up the stairs.

Tony—who owned the magazine stand to my left—studied the laws of probability because he likes to bet on the horse races. He claimed that he could calculate, according to his system, that if I held my job one hundred and twelve years more I would know everybody in the world by sight.

And I came to the theory that if you wait long enough in a big railroad station like Union Station you'll see everybody that travels.

I've told my theory to lots of people but nobody ever did anything about it except Harry. He came in a little over three years ago and waited at the head of the stairs for the passengers from the 9:05 train.

I remember seeing Harry that first evening. He wasn't much more than a thin, anxious kid then. He was all dressed up and I knew he was meeting his girl and that they would be married twenty minutes after she arrived. There's no use my trying to explain how I knew all this but after you've watched people waiting at the head of the stairs for eighteen years as I have done, then it is easy.

Well, the passengers came up and I had to get busy. I didn't look toward the stairs again until nearly time for the 9:18 and I was very much surprised to see that the young fellow was still there.

She didn't come on the 9:18 either, nor on the 9:40, and when the passengers from the 10:02 had all arrived and left, Harry was looking pretty desperate. Pretty soon he came close to my window so I called out and asked him what she looked like.

You would have thought that I had checked her among the packages in my check-room from the way he came over and half crawled through my window. "She's small and dark," he says, "and nineteen years old and very neat in the way she walks. She has a face," he says, thinking a minute, "that has lots of spirit. I mean she can get mad but she never stays mad for long. And her eyebrows come to a little point in the middle. She's got a brown fur, but maybe she isn't wearing it."

I couldn't remember seeing anybody like that.

He showed me the telegram he'd received: ARRIVE THURSDAY MEET ME STATION LOVE LOVE LOVE LOVE—MAY. It was from Omaha, Nebraska.

"Well," I finally says, "why don't you phone to your home? She's probably called there if she got in ahead of you."

He gave me a sick look, "I've only been in town two days. We were going to meet and then drive down South where I've got a job promised me. She—she hasn't any address for me." He touched the telegram. "I got this general delivery."

With that, he walked off to the head of the stairs to look over the people from the 11:22.

When I came on duty the next day he was still there and came over as soon as he saw me.

"Did she work anywhere?" I asked.

He nodded. "She was a typist. I telegraphed her

former boss. All they know is that she left her job to get married."

Well, that was how it began. Harry met every train for the next three or four days. Of course, the railroad lines made a routine check-up and the police looked into the case. But nobody was any real help. I could see that they all figured that May had simply played a trick on him. But I never believed that, somehow.

One day, after about two weeks, Harry and I were talking and I told him about my theory. "If you'll just wait long enough," I says, "you'll see her coming up those stairs some day." He turned and looked at the stairs as though he had never seen them before, while I went on explaining about Tony's figures on the Laws of Probability.

Next day when I came to work Harry was behind the counter of Tony's magazine stand. He looked at me rather sheepishly and says, "Well, I had to get a job somewhere, didn't I?"

So he began to work as a clerk for Tony. We never spoke of May any more and neither of us ever mentioned my theory. But I noticed that Harry always saw every person who came up the stairs.

Toward the end of the year Tony was killed in some argument over gambling, and Tony's widow left Harry in complete charge of the magazine stand. And when she got married again some time later, Harry bought the stand from her. He borrowed money and installed a soda fountain and pretty soon he had a very nice little business.

Then came yesterday. I heard a cry and a lot of things falling. The cry was from Harry and the things falling were a lot of dolls and other things which he had upset while he was jumping over the counter. He ran across and grabbed a girl not ten feet from my window. She was small and dark and her eyebrows came to a little point in the middle.

For a while they just hung there to each other laughing and crying and saying things without meaning. She'd say a few words like, "It was the bus station I meant—" and he'd kiss her speechless and tell her the many things he had done to find her. What apparently had happened three years before was that May had come by bus, not by train, and in her telegram she meant "bus station", not "railroad station". She had waited at the bus station for days and had spent all her money trying to find Harry. Finally she got a job typing.

"What?" says Harry. "Have you been working in town? All the time?"

She nodded.

"Well, Heavens—didn't you ever come down here to the station?" He pointed across to his magazine stand. "I've been there all the time. I own it. I've watched everybody that came up the stairs—"

She began to look a little pale. Pretty soon she looked over at the stairs and said in a weak voice, "I—I never came up the stairs before. You see, I went out of town yesterday on a short business trip—Oh, Harry!" Then she threw her arms around his neck and really began to cry.

After a minute she backed away and pointed very stiffly toward the north end of the station. "Harry, for three years, for three solid years, I've been right over there —working right in this very station, typing, in the office of the station-master."

The wonderful thing to me is how the Laws of Probability worked so hard and so long until they finally got May to walk up those stairs of ours.

Exercises for Conversation

A—Answer the Following:

1. By whom is this story narrated? 2. Why had Tony, who owned the magazine stand, made a study of the laws of probability? 3. Why had Harry first come to Union Station? 4. How was the check-room man, who tells the story, able to tell that Harry was waiting for his girl and that they were going to get married etc.? 5. For how many days did Harry continue to meet every train that arived? 6. Why was Harry unable to get in touch with May and why was she unable to get in touch with him? 7. Where did Harry finally get a job? 8. What happened when Tony, the owner of the magazine stand, died suddenly? 9. Did Harry succeed or fail in his business as owner of the magazine stand? 10. Did Harry cease to look for May or did he watch everyone who came up the stairs? 11. What cry and what noise did the check-man hear one day coming from the direction of Harry's magazine stand? 12. How was the check-room man able to recognize May immediately? 13. What station had May meant in her telegram of three years ago? 14. Where had May been working in the meantime? 15. Why had the fact that Union Station was so large and was used by so many people worked in Harry's disfavor as well as in his favor?

B—Give Sentences with the Following:

according to
by sight
all dressed up
pretty soon
to get mad
to look over
as soon as

to play a trick on
as though
in charge of
to get married
for a while
each other

C—Vocabulary Practice. Answer each of the following correctly:

1. In which of these can you best leave your packages for a while (railroad-station, magazine stand, check-room, bus station)?
2. Which of these verbs has the same form in the present and past tenses (do, know, bet, see, calculate)?
3. We use the word *mad* to describe a person who is insane and also one who is simply (small and dark, neat, excited, angry).
4. Which of these is the opposite of *borrow* (ask, lend, need, beg)?
5. Which of the following is an adverb: nice, always, law, notice?
6. With which of the following does the word *pretty* rhyme (ready, city, little, duty, lady)?
7. How many syllables does each of the following words contain: on which syllable do we accent each one (borrowed, pretty, probability, grabbed, apparently)?
8. Give the full form of the following contractions used in this story: you'll, didn't, couldn't, I've, she's, don't, he'd.
9. The opposite of *south* is (east, west, north, southwest).
10. What are the opposites of these words: thin, lend, before, more, many, dark, east?
11. What is the noun form of the verb *argue?* Of the verb *marry?*
12. To *grab* is to (install, wait, go up to, seize roughly).

THE BIG CHANCE

Frederick Laing

The Big Chance

Frederick Laing

He wasn't the kind to pick a secretary by the color of her hair. Not Bill Hargrave. Both Paula and Nancy had been smart enough to know that. And for some time everyone in the office had known that one of them, Paula or Nancy, was going to get the job. In fact, the decision would probably be made this afternoon. Hargrave was leaving town and wanted to settle the matter before he left.

The two girls could see him from their desks outside his office. Maybe it was only some correspondence that he was looking at with cool, keen eyes. But for a moment his finger seemed to pause above those two efficient little push-buttons. If he pressed the left one, it would be Paula's pulse which would begin to beat faster.

Paula couldn't keep her eyes off that light on her desk. She kept making mistakes in her typing and nervously taking the sheets of paper out in order to start all over again.

She leaned across her typewriter and said to Nancy "The boss is all dressed up today. He must be going on a special trip."

She was just talking to relieve her nervousness. Nancy took her time about answering. She wasn't used to having Paula talk to her in such an intimate tone. Not since they'd learned a month ago that they were both in line for a promotion, for the important job as Bill Hargrave's secretary.

"He does look nice."

Hargrave was young and outside of office hours he was said to be human. But that wasn't why he'd gotten to be one of the important officials of the company. He was quiet, and some of the other men in the office hadn't realized how fast he was succeeding in the company until they saw him one day in one of the top executive positions.

The two girls saw him get up from his desk and walk to the doorway of his office. He stood there with one hand in a pocket of his double-breasted blue flannel suit. There was a small white flower in his buttonhole and the usual keen, unrevealing smile on his face.

"Did you send for the tickets?" he asked Nancy.

"I got the tickets all right," she answered, "but" . . . and she tried to smile in the same hard way the boss did. She looked about as hardboiled as a white kitten. "But there just aren't any staterooms to be had," she told him. "Not for love nor money."

The boss was certainly disappointed. Anybody could see that.

"Suppose I try it?" Paula suggested quickly.

And for the next ten minutes, half the office employees could hear Paula telling the ticket-agent exactly what she thought of him.

"Listen," she said, "I don't care whose reservations you have to cancel . . ."

Well, the job was worth going after. There was the salary, for one thing. And there was the prestige. The boss' secretary knew a great deal about the business. And there were the interesting people she got to talk to. The important people. And the boxes of perfume, flowers and candy they often left on her desk.

And there was Bill Hargrave for a boss. Young and clever and attractive. That was a factor, too. Because in the advertising business you called the boss "Bill," and he called his secretary "Nancy" or "Paula", and took her to dinner on the company expense account.

It was all strictly business, but it seemed intimate and informal.

Both Paula and Nancy knew about those dinners. Bill had tried to be fair. He would ask Paula to stay one night, and then it would be Nancy's turn the next night.

But Paula had been smart. She had soon learned how impersonal Bill Hargrave could be, even at those intimate dinners. About as personal as one of those advertisements that says, "This means you." And she saw how much harder to please he was during the overtime hours—more irritable, more inclined to be critical in his manner.

So when Nancy had said, "I don't mind staying nights, really. I know Paula usually has a date. She's popular with the men . . ." well, Paula had been glad to let it go at that. She'd been quick to see that neither of them was going to get the job simply on a basis of physical attractiveness, and she was right.

Paula didn't need any lessons when it came to office politics. She was the one who was always busy when someone of little importance in the office wanted his material typed. "Sorry, but it's impossible, Jack. Why not ask Nancy."

And they did ask Nancy. It left Paula free to do Bill Hargrave's work in a hurry. She was never too busy for Mr. Bill's work.

When Hargrave finally pressed one of those buttons it was at Paula's desk that the light went on. She started to make a grab for her note book, but she quickly took out her mirror first. Then she grabbed up her note book and an envelope that was on the desk.

As for Nancy, what else could she do but sit there with her pretty blonde head bent over her typewriter? Nancy was a natural blonde, and that seemed the best way to describe her. She just didn't seem to know any tricks, such as Paula did, for making herself more popular with the boss.

The moment Paula got inside Hargrave's office, he asked about that stateroom.

"Any luck, Paula?"

Paula wasn't dumb. It was the little things that would count with Mr. Bill. Orchestra seats at the theatre when an important client was in town and the show was sold out. Or a stateroom when there were "no staterooms to be had for love nor money."

She handed him the envelope. It contained the two sets of tickets. "That's your stateroom number on the outside," she said in a business-like way.

She had on a double-breasted blue flannel suit something like Bill's, and it was clear he thought she looked pretty smart in it.

"Don't forget the time," she added, "eight-fifteen."

Hargrave smiled. "So there were no staterooms for love nor money, eh?"

He looked again at the number of his stateroom and he put the envelope carefully in his inside pocket.

Then he told her. She was going to have a new job. He mentioned the salary, too. He didn't neglect to mention the salary

She took it just right—in a very business-like manner. Just enough of gratitude. And then, the old sportsmanship. How sorry she felt about Nancy. She didn't look sorry.

And neither did Bill. He told her it was okay, that she shouldn't worry about Nancy, that Nancy wasn't made for the job anyway, and that, besides, he and Nancy were leaving on their honeymoon tonight. Tonight at eight-fifteen.

Exercises for Conversation

A—Answer these Questions:

1. What were the positions which Paula and Nancy held in the advertising company of this story? 2. Why was Paula very nervous this afternoon and why did she keep making so many mistakes as she typed? 3. What position were both of them very much interested in obtaining? 4. What were some of the advantages to be gained in being promoted to the position of Bill Hargrave's secretary? 5. How did the two girls, Paula and Nancy, differ in their characters? 6. Which was the more efficient of the two girls? 7. Why was Paula always busy when some of the men of lesser importance in the office wanted her to do some typing for them? 8. Are you yourself able or unable to type well? 9. Which of the two girls was finally able to obtain tickets for the stateroom for Bill Hargrave for that evening? 10. Which of the girls did Bill Hargrave finally select to be his secretary in the future? Which did he select as his wife?

B—Give Sentences with the Following:

for some time
in fact
to leave town
to keep one's eye on something
to be dressed up
to take one's time
to be used to
to go after
to be in a hurry

C—Vocabulary Practice. Answer each of the following correctly:

1. To *pick* a secretary is to (criticize one, select one, admire one, promote one).
2. To *settle* a matter is to (consider it, set it aside, decide it, postpone it).
3. *Keen* means (sharp, dull, late, easy).
4. What is the opposite of the following: fast, important, top, efficient, quickly.
5. To *cancel* something is to (put it off, call it off, put it away, put it down).
6. Which of these will make you smell sweet (candy, stateroom, perfume, mirror)?
7. What is the past tense form of these verbs: to try, to take, to leave, to see, to bend?
8. How many syllables does each of the following words contain: material, grabbed, typewriter, naturally, seemed, typed, counted?
9. Which of these is a material often used to make men's suits (salary, flannel, expense-account, pride)?
10. A *kitten* is a (ticket-agent, boss, good salary, young cat).
11. A *great deal* is a (little, lot, necessity, state room).
12. What is the full form of each of the following contractions: don't, didn't, she'd, wasn't, it's, she's, they'd?

TEN STEPS

Robert Littell

Ten Steps

Robert Littell

I put on a clean collar. I was in our room on the second floor where I could see into the Hubbells' yard, and the ring on the stone post where they tie up their dog. The dog wasn't there. The collar which I took off had two kinds of laundry marks on the inside, one mark from the laundry where I used to take my shirts and a second mark from the present laundry. Then I washed my hands.

The soap was worn down so that there was almost none left. It was a soap that smelled like salad. I turned off the water, but the water still went drip-drip from the faucet. I dried my hands. I hung the towel on the left end of the rod. The right end of the rod is for Mae. The rod is glass, and some day it will come loose and fall down and break. I shut the bathroom door so that I would not hear the drip-drip of the water from the faucet.

I went into the room again which is Mae's and mine. On her bed in the daytime she keeps a French doll with big eyes. Where the back of the bed hits the wall there is a mark. I moved out the bed, and I saw the mark. It is black, and a yard long. The doll fell off and I put it back on the bed so it could not look at me when I went out. Then I went out.

I was in the hall, and I shut my eyes. I did not know what kind of wallpaper there was in the hall. I thought that it would be green, but when I opened my eyes again it was more blue than green, with a woman, and a basket and a lamb. Around the door the paper was cut off, and there was only the lamb; eight times, from the ceiling to the floor, no woman, and no basket, but only the lamb. I could touch the ceiling when I stood on my toes.

Next to our room is the extra room, which we do not use. I went into that. The back of the mirror was peeling off, and both windows were closed. On the window there was a large fly, and I opened the window and drove him out and he flew away; and in the window frame there was a long nail, and I took off my shoe and drove in the nail with the heel of my shoe. Then I put on my shoe again. I measured the room by walking across it in each direction from one wall to the other. It is ten by fourteen.

I came into the parlor from the door across from the desk. The desk has three drawers down one side. I took out an envelope from the bottom drawer and put some money in it and wrote "For Mae" on it and put it on the top of the desk. The curtains in the parlor were red. Where the sun hits them there is a part that is not red, but pink. There was a magazine on the table called *Movieland,* and I started to read it, but I did not read it. I went over to the fireplace and looked at the rest of the room from there, and I saw the table and the carpet and how two chairs were facing right toward each other. I sat down on one of them and one of its legs was shorter than the others and I got up and went into the kitchen.

In the kitchen I saw Mae shelling peas. She forced the peas out of the shell with her thumb and they fell into the bowl. There were three peas on the floor and I picked them up and put them in my pocket. The kitchen floor was laid in linoleum with blue and white squares two inches square. Mae was sitting on a stool, reading a paper placed in front of her. She did not turn around when I came in. She said, "When you come back bring some stove-polish with you."

There was a pan on the stove and steam was coming from it. The stove had places for six pans. Two of the places had smaller rings inside of them for smaller pans. Mae said:

"They found Matthews doubled up inside his car. He had bled to death. The bullet went through his left lung and he bled to death."

Mae was looking at the paper and shelling peas. The sun was on part of the paper and she moved it a little. Then she said, "I suppose you're going now."

I said I was going now.

I went out through the back door into the yard. There I saw my kid playing with some sand and toys in the sand. He was putting the sand into a toy truck, and then running the truck back and forth through the sand. The sand was wet, and I could see the print of his hand on it. It was his left hand. I said, "So long, son," to him, but he didn't say anything. He was too busy with his truck and the sand.

Then I went to the garage, and unlocked the door. I ran a cloth over the windshield of the car, and it was scratched in a half circle where the windshield wiper wipes it. And I stood there for a couple of minutes, and then I closed the doors, and walked along outside of the house to the front and looked at my watch. It was twenty minutes to ten.

Then I walked down the wooden steps to the sidewalk, and I counted the steps. I counted ten steps, I thought I counted the last step, but perhaps I didn't. I walked down the street, and looked back, and saw the house, and there was one window with a shade halfway down, and I wanted to go back and count the steps again to make sure, but I didn't. I walked down to the corner and took the street-car and got off at the police-station and found Captain Rogers and told him that if they were looking for the man who killed Sam Matthews they should arrest me because I had done it.

Captain Rogers asked me if I wanted to write out a confession and I said that I would, but before I tell them how I killed Matthews I want to write down the last things which I saw in my house and how I remember them, because now I'll want always to be able to remember about all those things that I won't ever see again, maybe.

Exercises for Conversation

A—Answer these Questions:

1. To what ten steps does the person who tells this story refer in the title? 2. What crime had he committed? 3. What were some of the things which he did before giving himself up to the police? 4. What was his purpose in observing so carefully some of the minor things in his home? 5. What was his wife doing when he went into the kitchen? 6. What did she ask him to bring back with him when he came home again? 7. What was his son doing in the back yard? 8. What did he do when he went to the garage? 9. Did he take his car out of the garage or did he leave it there? 10. Why did he run a cloth over the windshield of the car? 11. Did he drive to the police station in his car or did he go by street-car? 12. What did he say to the police captain when he entered the police station? 13. Do you find this story interesting and realistic or a little absurd? 14. To what extent do you consider this story well-written? To what extent do you consider it poorly written?

B—Give Sentences with the Following:

to put on
to take off
to wear down
to turn off
to fall down (off, over)
to cut off
to peel off
to take out
to go out
to pick up
to turn around
to write down

C—Vocabulary Practice. Answer the following correctly:

1. Which of these is the opposite of to *put on* (put away, take away, take down, take off)?
2. To which of the following do we send dirty clothing to be washed (police-station, garage, kitchen, laundry)?
3. When water leaks slowly from a faucet we say that it (rushes, drips, whispers, bangs).
4. Little girls like to play with (dolls, trucks, wallpaper, peas).
5. A young sheep is a (lamb, calf, colt).
6. Two important parts of a shoe are the *sole* and the (stool, hole, heel, desk).
7. We often cover the floors of our kitchens with (nails, sand, linoleum, squares).
8. The outer covering of an apple or an orange is called the (heel, fireplace, step, peel).
9. Which of the following is a past participle: saw, taken, find, went?
10. With which of the following does the word *bled* rhyme (seed, said, set, sad)?
11. A gun generally contains (legs, peas, stove-polish, bullets).
12. In what two different ways may the word *rest* be used?

DECISION

Roy Hilligoss

Decision

Roy Hilligoss

Even after a year, Chad still called us Aunt Pat and Uncle Bill. But we thought our job had become that of mother and father—until that letter arrived from the 6th artillery headquarters in North Africa to our mailbox in East Orange, New Jersey.

Chad had come to us an English refugee. He was supposed to stay until they had put "Mr. Hitler in the bag," as he expressed it, and he could go back to his adored father, Major Jollison of the Royal Artillery. In other words, he had been sent to the United States like many other English children to live with an American family for the duration of the war, after which time he planned to return home to London.

But Major Jollison had been killed while resisting a Nazi tank attack in the North African desert.

Chad had taken the news without the slightest show of emotion. Probably Pat and I alone realized the sharp pain that must have torn through his young heart when he learned that his father was dead. He was English and his people were fighting a desperate battle, so he could not let his own individual tragedy show.

England meant much to him too, but when he had recovered a little from the shock he seemed resigned to living with us and becoming an American. He had had no one else but his father.

"I shall try very hard," he told us seriously in that

thin, rather sharp voice of his, "to be as you would want your own boy to be. I shall get onto your American ways as quickly as I can and try to make you quite proud of me." He smiled. "I shall even admire your Revolutionary patriots."

So we couldn't help loving him, you see, and hoping he really wanted to stay with us forever, even after the war had ended.

He did brilliantly, and an early problem—the way the other boys at school kidded him about his English accent and manners—had disappeared. Everyone in town knew how bravely his father had died, and this gave Chad a certain romantic interest.

In fact, everything had gone beautifully—till that letter came from a member of the 6th artillery, Captain Burroughs. The 6th artillery had been Major Jollison's military unit.

Pat held the letter out to me one evening, the moment I came in the door. But she was too upset emotionally to wait until I'd read it.

"He was terribly fond of Chad's father, Bill," she said. "And he'd like to offer Chad a place to live—with his mother in her home just outside London."

I looked up from the letter. "He says he recognizes the danger."

"But he's like all Englishmen, I suppose," Pat said. "Rain or shine, bombs or no bombs, they think that England is the only place in the world to live. And of course he thinks Chad will be company for his mother. She's old and alone. . . . Oh, Bill, do you think he'll go?"

I shook my head. "I don't know. But I've been afraid he would some day."

"But he has no relatives there. Surely he'd rather be with us. . . ."

"It's like you said—rain or shine. And he's not really our boy, Pat; we just hoped he would be, and he's tried to pretend."

She sighed. "I know. I was only hoping, not talking sense. Well . . ." she took my arm, "—let's go up to his room and tell him."

Chad was lying on his small stomach, reading, when we entered his room. He got quickly to his feet and shook my hand—he always did that when I got home evenings. "How'd the stock-market go today, Uncle Bill?" He was picking up our ways fast.

I handed him the letter.

I watched his blue eyes move quickly back and forth across the page, and when they reached the bottom they stayed there. He was thinking rapidly. Suddenly I knew he'd made his decision because his face lost all expression: a habit of his.

"Are you going, dear?" Pat asked softly.

He nodded. "I must, Aunt Pat."

"They're raining bombs on London, old son," I said.

"I know," he said. "That's why I'm going."

"I don't understand," I said.

"I mean . . ." for a moment he paused "—well, when your country's having its most difficult times, that's when it needs you most."

That sounded a bit too grown-up, too like something he had read somewhere. I looked suspiciously at him, but his eyes met mine bravely. "All right, old son," I said. "I'm sorry, but if you. . . ."

"I'm sorry too," he said quickly. "Really, Uncle Bill. But I must go."

"I'd better finish getting dinner," Pat said in a queer voice, and left us.

"And I have to wash," Chad said steadily.

I was left, staring down at the letter from Captain Burroughs, already missing this strange youngster as if he'd been all our own from the very start.

We didn't talk much about his going. But we might as well have discussed it constantly; it certainly was with us every moment. From that first night, on through the week following, there were few signs of cheerfulness in our house.

But the evening I came home with final details about his trip to New York, where a friend of mine would take charge and get him safely onto the boat . . . well, that about finished it. Chad's quiet, unrevealing face didn't change a bit, but Pat looked at me as if I'd struck her. I knew how she felt.

Late that night I woke up, frightened, sure I had heard Chad crying in the next room. But it was Pat.

"You're crying, darling?"

"Of course," she said shakily. "Oh, Bill, it hurts to lose him."

I held her close. "I know so well," I said. "He's like our own boy."

And then so quickly, it was the day for Chad to leave us. I had stayed home to drive him to the station, but Pat wasn't going along. She said she simply couldn't take it.

The three of us were standing in the doorway, just standing there with little to say. Chad was wearing the same clothes he had come to America in—he had wanted to wear them—the short coat, the small cap, the wool stockings that left his knees bare. But when we had first seen him, on a dock in New York, he had been looking about him defiantly, with his chin out, trying to hide his fears; now his face was serious, his lower lip pulled slightly in.

"I've been happy here," he said.

He was interrupted by the mailman, who handed a letter to Pat. She passed it on to me.

"Goodbye, Chad," she said weakly. "Always remember that we. . . ."

"Wait," I broke in. "This letter's from Captain Burroughs." But my enthusiasm was short-lived. "It's just a little consolation," I said. He says we won't have to worry about Chad. Mrs. Burroughs is being removed to Australia and Chad is supposed to join her there. There won't be any bombs anyway."

"That's something," Pat said.

But Chad was suddenly all animation. "Then I don't have to go!"

Pat dropped to her knees and stared at him. "You don't have to go? Didn't you want to go?"

"Why, no," Chad said. "But she was a very old lady and all alone in the bombings. I thought I would be able to protect her. But now that she's been sent to Australia. . . ."

"Why on earth didn't you tell us how you felt?" I demanded.

He seemed a little embarrassed. "I was afraid," he said, "that it might seem forward of me to think I could protect Mrs. Burroughs. And I knew you wouldn't want a son who was forward."

Pat was half laughing, half crying, and hugging him wildly. To cover my own feelings, I said with an imitation English accent, "Then you're quite happy now, old boy?"

"Quite happy?" He smiled up at me. "Uncle Bill, I feel like a million bucks!"

Chad Jollison—American schoolboy, our boy.

Exercises for Conversation

A—Answer the Following:

1. Why had Chad left England and come to live with an American family? 2. What had happened to Chad's father? 3. Why were Pat and Bill very disappointed to receive the letter from Captain Burroughs, the friend of Chad's father? 4. What offer did Captain Burroughs make to Chad in his letter? 5. After reading Captain Burroughs' letter why did Chad decide immediately to return to England? 6. Were Pat and Bill happy or unhappy about Chad's decision? 7. Why didn't Pat wish to go to the station with Bill to see Chad off? 8. What letter arrived just as Chad and Bill were about to leave? 9. To what country, according to the letter, was Captain Burroughs' mother being removed? 10. Why was she being removed to Australia? 11. Why did Chad now feel that he was relieved of the obligation to return to England? 12. What did Chad mean when he said that he felt "like a million bucks"?

B—Give Sentences with the Following:

in other words
to *kid* someone
in fact
to go well
to be upset
to be fond of
of course
rain or shine
to had better do something
to wake up
to break in
to feel like a million (bucks)

C—Vocabulary Practice. Answer each of the following correctly:

1. Which of these is an officer in the army (private, major, patriot, refugee)?

2. Which of these verbs has the same form in the present and past tenses (tear, let, try, resign)?

3. Which of these do you eat at the conclusion of your meal—*desert* or *dessert?*

4. What is the adjective form of the noun *tragedy?* Of the noun *enthusiasm?*

5. What is the noun form of the verb *admire?*

6. To *kid* is to (applaud, adore, throw stones at, make fun of).

7. If a person is very *upset,* he is (hungry, upside down, down and out, emotionally disturbed).

8. Which two of the following words rhyme with the word *sigh* (tie, say, see, cry, dig)?

9. What are the full forms of the following contractions, as used in this story (couldn't, he'd, it's, let's, he'll, how'd, they're, I've)?

10. A *bit* means (a great deal, a lot, a little, enough).

11. If I do something *constantly,* I do it (seldom, off and on, now and then, continuously).

12. What are the opposites of these words: lower, weakly few, short-lived?

13. One *hugs* a person by (kissing him, criticizing him, smiling at him, throwing one's arms around him).

14. To *pretend* is to (break in, make believe, take off, put up with).

FINAL BREAK

Ian S. Thompson

Final Break

Ian S. Thompson

They had been walking along Oxford Street, now they stopped, Greg's hand on her arm.

"This is the place," he said. "I thought you might get the sort of thing you liked here."

Helen nodded, but there were tears in her eyes as she looked through the shop-window. The new hat had been his idea, not hers.

"What about that black one?" He pointed. "It would go with your suit!"

Her lips trembled. One of the little things she loved so much about him was the really genuine interest he had always taken in what she wore. It had made you feel young somehow, loved, though in your heart you knew you were young no longer.

"Yes. Yes, it would, wouldn't it?" She carefully avoided meeting his eyes, because there was so much in her own eyes that he must never see.

They went into the shop. A clerk appeared to wait upon them.

Helen described the hat. It was in the window.

She was wishing now that they had never come into the shop. But Greg had been insistent. He wanted to give her something. A parting gift, he had called it.

He was smiling now out of blue, untroubled eyes. Which surprised her. And yet why should it, she asked herself, as she took the hat from the clerk and placed it on her blue-grey hair? She had always tried to be modern, and part of modernity was to see these things through bravely, when and if they came.

Her mind turned back. And she saw herself in the hat-shop mirror, not as someone in a black tailored suit, but as a bride. Smiling, radiant, on Greg's arm. At least they had said she had looked that. She had never thought of it, never cared. She had been so completely, so blindly happy.

Five minutes later they were out again in the sunshine of the street and Greg, after looking at his watch, suggested tea.

"I know a place—" There was an expression of excitement in his eyes which she could not understand. "You'll like it there."

It was a small, very ordinary café in one of the side streets off Oxford Street. He ordered for them both, and then leaned back.

He didn't speak, but his hand came out across the table and took hers.

"Please, God, don't let me cry," she prayed. "Not now. Not so long as he's with me."

The tea arrived. He drank one cup quickly, lit himself a cigarette, and then said:

"You're quite certain that you want to stay on in that house alone? I mean—well, I feel rather badly about the whole thing, and if there's anything I could do—"

There was one thing, but it would have been hysterical weakness to have suggested it. She shook her head. She didn't want him to have any feelings of regret, any pains of conscience. It had been wonderful having him for all those years.

"No, really," she said. "It'll be all right."

But he still didn't seem satisfied.

"There's another thing I'd like to mention," he said. "I didn't say anything about it before because I know—well, I know how sensitive you are about that sort of thing—" He broke off and then went hurriedly on, his eyes avoiding hers. "It's money. I've arranged with the bank. . . ."

The color came at once to her cheeks. Not because of any false pride. That was a luxury you couldn't afford if you had no one to support you. But—

"Oh, Greg, you shouldn't," she said with embarrassment.

He brushed that aside. Angrily almost.

"Why not? It's something I want to do. And Sandra—" He mentioned the girl's name—"she agrees. We were talking about it last night."

Sandra. . . . We. . . . How easily, familiarly, he spoke of her, Helen thought with an ache. And yet two months ago they hadn't even met. Two months. . . . Was it really only that time since he'd gone up to London on that business trip?

She had realized, of course, after he came back that there was something, although he hadn't actually said a word then. Some deep-rooted woman's instinct had warned her that he wasn't all hers any longer, that she was sharing him with someone else.

A girl. Young, fresh, and lovely. The imagined picture had filled her with a sense of panic. He had changed his job for a better one and gone up to live in London. For a month she hadn't seen him. And she had never met the girl.

Sandra . . . She worked in the advertising business, he had told her. And very clever. But that didn't matter to Helen. When you have loved somebody with every part of you, you did not think of cleverness in considering that younger person to whom you were losing him.

Was she really nice? Would she work to keep him happy as you had tried to do?

But Sandra. . . . The name had a sharp quality. You couldn't imagine a girl with a name like that being—Helen's eyes were drawn to a girl who had just walked into the café, who was looking around hesitantly—well like that, for instance.

Then the girl turned. She was beautiful, with a shy, sweet loveliness that caught at your heart. Helen stared, quite unconscious that she was staring. And then her eyes widened in surprise as she saw Greg rise to his feet. The girl was hurrying towards their table.

"So you were able to get here, darling!" She heard Greg's voice and then he had turned, was smiling down at her. "A litle surprise," he said. "This is Sandra, Mother. Tomorrow's happy bride!"

Exercises for Conversation

A—Answer these Questions:

1. What is the significance of the title "Final Break" in this story? 2. Who is Greg? Who is Helen? 3. Why is Greg so attentive to Helen? 4. To what extent do you sympathize with Helen in this story? 5. Why does Greg insist on providing Helen with money for the future? 6. Which of these adjectives do you think best describes Helen as a mother: generous, possessive, unselfish, modern? 7. How had Greg first met Sandra? 8. Had Helen, Greg's mother, ever met Sandra previously? 9. Why does the author say that the imagined picture of Sandra filled Helen with panic? 10. What kind of

girl did Helen expect Sandra to be, judging only by her name and by her own personal emotions? 11. Where does the meeting between Helen and Sandra take place? 12. Why is Helen greatly surprised when she finally meets Sandra? 13. Do you feel that the author of this story tricked you in any way in leading up to his surprise ending or do you think that he presented all of the facts clearly? 14. Did you suspect that Helen was Greg's mother? If so, when?

B—Give Sentences with the Following:

to walk along	at least
what about	to lean back
to take an interest in	to break off
to wait upon	to brush aside
to see something through	to share with
to turn back	to look around

C—Vocabulary Practice. Answer each of the following correctly:

1. A person *nods,* slightly moving his (hand, finger, head, leg).
2. A person points, generally using his (finger, elbow, knee, neck).
3. If her lips *trembled,* they (were blue, needed lipstick, shook slightly, were cold).
4. A *shop* is a (café, small store, a genuine interest, a weakness).
5. A *parting* gift is one given when a person (graduates, has an important part in something, goes away, reaches 21).
6. In every marriage the man is referred to as the *groom* and the girl is called the ______.
7. What is the noun form of the adjective *exciting?* Of the adjective *happy?*
8. With which of the following does the word *ache* rhyme (catch, edge, make, ash)?
9. It *didn't matter* to her means that (she did not like it, it was not important to her, she was not surprised).

10. *For instance* means (for good, for example, forever, for nothing).

11. What is the past tense of each of these verbs: to smile, to draw, to lose, to break, to get, to make?

12. The opposite of *dull* is (boring, happy, sharp, smiling).

RED BALLOONS

Elmer Davis

Red Balloons

Elmer Davis

Lundy told himself afterward that he had been tempted beyond his strength. In fact he had never been really tempted before, for he had never had such an opportunity. He had gone to the bank—the branch bank in the poor, run-down neighborhood to which he had recently moved—to cut a coupon from his last bond; all the rest of his bonds and his money he had lost in his crazy attempt to make money on the stock-market so that he could give up his job and live in Florida. He took his safe-deposit box to one of the booths where people shut themselves in while they open their safe-deposit boxes in order to cut coupons or to put in or remove valuables. The booth had just been vacated by a fat woman wearing many jewels who had left it covered with torn papers.

A little annoyed, Lundy brushed away the torn papers —and came upon an envelope filled with money which the fat woman had obviously overlooked. A bank failure in the town had recently frightened many people; the fat woman looked like the sort of person who would turn her bank balance into cash and lock it up in her safe-deposit box. Lundy half opened the door to call her back and saw her walking out of the bank. Quickly he shut the door, counted the money. Nearly thirty thousand dollars; enough to keep a man comfortably, in some little Florida town, for the rest of his life.

Quickly, Lundy slipped the envelope into his inside pocket.

Then he left the bank, crossing the street into a little park with a high iron fence around it. It was, he knew, a private park, the possession of the old families that had once lived on the square; at night its gates were locked, a watchman guarded it. But by day it was open to all. He sat down on a bench, trembling in the winter wind; the envelope in his pocket felt like a piece of hot metal.

What a fool he had been! He had thought when he took it that it wouldn't be missed for a month—not until the woman came again to cut coupons. But if she kept all her money in her safe-deposit box she might come back and find it missing tomorrow—this afternoon. The bank employees would remember Lundy—he had recently rented his safe-deposit box; they might remember that he had followed her into the booth. If he gave up his job now and left for Florida, that would be a confession. But tonight, tomorrow, he might be questioned, his rooms examined. Where could he hide the money?

His throat was dry; he got up, walked to the center of the park, where he had seen a drinking fountain. Unable to decide what to do, he stared at the drinking fountain, at its tall concrete base. Then his eyes narrowed; the base was broken on one side—a hole big enough to put your hand through. Inside, there was a dark space where no one would think of looking for anything; where a man who had hidden something could come back and get it almost any time.

Beside the drinking fountain, Lundy kneeled down; anyone who had passed would have seen only a man with an unbuttoned overcoat hanging loose about him, kneeling down, tying his shoe. But when he went on, the envelope of money no longer lay like a piece of hot metal in his pocket. He had hidden it in the hole at the base of the drinking fountain.

That evening two detectives from police headquarters came to see him, to question him very politely and he met them smiling.

"Why, yes," he said. "There was a fat woman in the booth just before me; she left it covered with torn pieces of paper and I brushed them aside into the waste-paper basket. Find out where the waste-paper basket went, and you'll probably find the money. . . . No, I've no objection at all if you want to look around here, just to satisfy yourselves."

Afterward he wondered whether he had not overdone it. They went away apparently convinced, but he couldn't feel safe. He better leave the money where it was, for a while. There wasn't a chance in a million that anyone would look into the broken drinking fountain. There was no hope of his recovering the money at night; the park gate was locked; the watchman was on duty. Someday, when no one was near, he would kneel down as if to tie his shoe—

As he entered the park next morning, he saw something like a red cloud just above the drinking fountain. A red warning of danger. He became very nervous but then saw that it was only a group of toy balloons held by an old man. Lundy had never seen anyone selling balloons here in the three weeks in which he lived nearby; business couldn't be good, the old man would soon leave. But when Lundy came back at evening, he was still there in the same spot near the drinking fountain.

Lundy looked at him in passing; he was old but he looked strong. He might be a younger man in disguise—

not a seller of balloons; he might be a detective placed there to watch him. Lundy went home trembling. No one could have seen him put the money away—but suppose that by some accident the money had been found. The police would know the thief must come back for it; thus they had left a man on guard. *But had they left the money there in order to trap him?*

The next morning the balloon-seller was still there. That day Lundy went to the bank and risked a question. No, said the manager of the bank, they hadn't found the money; but they expected to find it. It seemed to Lundy that the manager looked at him in a rather suspicious manner.

That evening he spoke, in passing, to the balloon-seller.

"You work late, eh? Business must be good."

"Not so good. But I stay around until they lock the gates each night and the watchman arrives to guard the place."

There was not a moment then when the fountain was not being watched. That was the first night that Lundy could not sleep. In the morning the red cloud was still there, hanging above his treasure.

Well, if business was bad, the balloon-seller would soon leave and go somewhere else to sell his balloons. Lundy waited three more days, in which he saw, morning and evening, that red sign of danger. He couldn't stand this much longer: a balloon-seller, staying in a place where Lundy had never seen one before, couldn't be a balloon-seller. But, there was one chance, if the police had left the money. Policemen in uniform seldom came here; Lundy could wait for his chance until there was no one around, attack the balloon-seller, knock him out, take the money and escape before anyone came.

And so he waited his chance, found the old man alone, walked up to him, pretended to buy a balloon, then hit him, straight and hard, on the jaw. Down went the old man—down and out; down went Lundy on his knees, his arm reaching into the hole at the base of the fountain.

Up into the air went a dozen red balloons, released from the old man's hand as he fell; a dozen sudden red danger signals which could be seen everywhere in the park and from the nearby streets as well. As Lundy rose, pushing the money into his pocket, he saw a policeman coming up; he turned only to face another, tried to walk away coolly—

"Here!" said the policeman. "What's the matter with old Joe?"

"I don't know. I've done nothing." But the balloon man was talking now, explaining to the policeman what had happened. The policeman turned toward Lundy, severe.

"What's the idea of knocking down an old man that's just out of the hospital?"

"Just out of the hospital?" Lundy asked.

"Sure. He's been sick for a month. Haven't you noticed that for the past month he hasn't been here, at his regular place near the fountain. First time he's been away for twenty years. . . . Here, you—take your hand out of that pocket! Oh, it isn't a gun? Just papers? Well, come along with me and show them to the captain in the police headquarters."

Exercises for Conversation

A—Answer these Questions:

1. For what purpose had Lundy, the principal character of this story, gone to the bank this day? 2. Did Lundy have many or few bonds left from which to cut coupons? 3. How had he lost all his money? 4. Had he moved to this neighborhood recently or long ago? 5. What did the fat lady leave behind her in the booth? 6. Did she leave the envelope of money intentionally or was it something that she had overlooked? 7. Approximately how much money was there in the envelope? 8. Where did Lundy go when he left the bank? 9. Why did he think it would be unwise for him to give up his job right away and go to Florida? 10. Why was he afraid to take the money home with him? 11. Where did he finally hide the money? 12. What story did he tell the two detectives who came to visit him that evening? 13. What strange sight did he see the next morning when he visited the park? 14. Who did Lundy suspect the old balloon-seller to be? 15. What trap did he begin to think the police had set for him? 16. What happened when Lundy finally attacked the old man and knocked him down? 17. Why had the old man been absent from the park during the previous three weeks? 18. Why did Lundy have to accompany the policeman to police headquarters?

B—Give Sentences with the Following:

in fact	at all
to give up something	to look around
to come upon	to put something away
to lock up	to wait for
to kneel down	to be the matter with
to find out	to knock somebody down (out)

C—Vocabulary Practice. Answer the following correctly:

1. To *frighten* is to (relieve, adjust, scare, balance).
2. A man whose duty it is to guard a building each night is generally called a (banker, watchman, sergeant, thief).
3. What is the noun form of the verb *to confess?*
4. Which of these do we generally find in a park (detectives, benches, balloons, gates)?
5. What is the past tense form and the past participial form of these verbs: to hide, to give, to kneel, to tie, to help?
6. Which of these is a good place to keep valuables (pillow, hole, base of a drinking fountain, safe-deposit box)?
7. Which of these is a part of the body (pocket, headquarters, booth, knee)?
8. Which of these words is not spelled correctly (fountin, employee, confession, satisfy)?
9. Which of these is a synonym for the word *thief* (captain, robber, bank-employee, watchman)?
10. What is the opposite of the word *able?* Of the word *polite?* Of the verbs *to tie* and *to button?*
11. What is the adverb form of these adjectives: probable, apparent, polite, fast, quick, hard?
12. To *lock* something, one generally needs a (key, money, friends, waste-paper basket).

BETTER LATE

Edward Stevenson

Better Late

Edward Stevenson

Well, I'm certainly glad you're not seasick. When I first saw you leaning over the rail I said to myself that you must be seasick, though I couldn't see how anybody could get seasick with the water so calm the way it is today. Our room steward says that anybody that gets seasick in this kind of weather wouldn't be safe on the lake in Central Park. He's a regular comedian. . . . And that reminds me, how much do you think I ought to tip him—the room steward, I mean? I'm not a person who has a lot of money, but still I want to do the right thing as to tipping.

You see, this is the first time we've been on a boat—my wife and I, I mean. Of course we've taken a trip up the Hudson with the kids, but I guess you wouldn't mention the Hudson River Day Line in the same breath with a big ship like this, would you? The kids thought it was wonderful, though. They're grown up and married now, with kids of their own—except Judy, that is, and she hardly has had time, not having been married a year yet—but it doesn't seem more than yesterday that they were running around like wild Indians and getting into all kinds of trouble. Time certainly flies. . . .

Whew! It's getting hot, isn't it? We must be coming into the tropics from the way it feels. Ever been down here before, Mr.— I don't think you mentioned your name, did you? Arthur? Well, I'm glad to know you, Mr. Arthur My name's Bentham. I'd like you to meet my wife some time, too. That's my wife sitting in that deck chair down at the end. She's making believe she's reading that book, but she's sound asleep. The salt air seems to make her very tired. . . .

As I was saying, time certainly flies. Now, you take me, why, it seems only the other day that Ellen and I were getting married; and here we are grandparents of six already.

We've been married thirty-five years. It doesn't seem possible, but that's what it is, all right. Why, say, I can remember the wedding just as clearly as if it happened last week. It wasn't much of a wedding—you know, no ceremony and reception. Besides Ellen and me and the minister there were only the minister's wife and the church janitor, for witness. But I can still see the five of us standing there in the chapel, with the sun coming through a high window and falling around us and turning everything golden. I remember Ellen especially. She was so pretty and little. Lord, I felt big and awkward beside her.

Will you look at them flying fish! Aren't they the funny things?

When I look back, I think that Ellen and I must have been crazy, getting married the way we did. My goodness, I didn't have a cent to my name—it was all I could do to get together the money for the wedding ring. Engagement rings and honeymoons and all those special things were out of reach as far as we were concerned.

I felt pretty bad, taking her right from church to a $2.50-a-week furnished room. A wonderful girl like her deserved better, and I told her so. A big wedding, a reception at the Hotel Waldorf—the old Waldorf, you know—and a honeymoon at Niagara Falls was little enough for her. But she just laughed. "If I wanted such foolishness,' she says, "I'd have married Mr. Astor and not Johnny Bentham." That's the way she is. I didn't mind so much not having a big church wedding, or a reception afterwards, but, gee, what's a wedding without a honeymoon? I mean, it made me feel rather low, not being able to provide even that.

You know, marrying Ellen was the making of me. I was just a shipping clerk at the time, but she made me study bookkeeping and when an opening in the company came along I stepped right into it. I'm head bookkeeper now. Of course that isn't so much—there's only one other bookkeeper—but being head of anything is pretty good these days, I always say. A couple of years back when I'd been with the company thirty-five years they put on a dinner for me at Jack Dempsey's Restaurant and gave me a watch. Here it is. See what it says, "To John W. Bentham"—that's my full name—"for thirty-five years of devoted service. Atlas Paper & Supply Co." Mr. Stover, the president, made a speech. I did too—but I was too choked up to say much. You can bet that I'd never have stayed in that company long enough to get that watch if it hadn't been for Ellen.

And the kids, too, of course. When you get to be a family man you have to be a little more serious. Kit—that's short for Christopher—was the first; then Roger, Cynthia, Anthony, and Judy, the baby. Nice names, aren't they? Ellen picked them out.

They're all grown up now—fine young men and women, if I do say so myself—but there were times when you just wondered if they ever would grow up. It was just one thing after another. Sick or healthy, they had you up to your neck in bills.

Is that land over there to the left? No, I guess it's just clouds.

Well, last year our company did pretty well and they gave all the old employees a month's pay for a bonus at Christmas—first bonus we had had in years. So what did I do? Well, I figured with all the kids married and no one to take care of but ourselves, that we didn't have any real need for the money, so I didn't breathe a word about it to Ellen. You see, I'd been seeing those cruise advertisements in the papers and I thought to myself that's just the thing for Ellen and me. Twelve days. Nassau, Jamaica, and Cuba. $125 and up. I didn't say anything till about two weeks before we were about to sail. Then I broke the news. Well you could have knocked Ellen over with a feather.

"Johnny Bentham," she says, "are you out of your mind?"

"No," I says. "And I haven't robbed a bank, either." So I told her all about the bonus.

Well, she still thought I was crazy. "Spending all that money on a little trip," she says. "Do you think we're millionaires? Johnny, I'll never put foot on that boat."

"Now that's a fine way to feel!" I says, acting as if I were insulted. "A woman refusing to go on a honeymoon with her husband!"

Well, she just looked at me and I just looked at her, and first thing you know she threw her arms around me and began kissing me, and what did the two of us do but end up laughing and crying like a couple of kids.

"Gee, Mama," I says. "It's better late than never, isn't it?" . . .

Say, look at those flying fish. . . .

Exercises for Conversation

A—Answer these Questions:

1. How many characters actually speak in this story? 2. Had Mr. Bentham, who tells the story, ever been on a boat previously? 3. Who was accompanying Mr. Bentham on this boat trip? 4. Had Mr. and Mrs. Bentham been married only previously or many years ago? 5. Judging by the references to Central Park, the Hudson River, and the Hotel Waldorf, in what city would you say that Mr. and Mrs. Bentham lived? 6. Had the marriage of Mr. and Mrs. Bentham been a very simple or a very elaborate affair? 7. Why had they been unable to go on a honeymoon at the time? 8. What kind of work was Mr. Bentham doing when he got married? 9. Why does he say that his wife, Ellen, was the "making" of him? 10. What position, according to Mr. Bentham, does he now hold in the company? 11. At the end of his thirty-five years of devoted service to the company, how did the company honor him? 12. How did Mr. Bentham unexpectedly get the money to take this cruise? 13. To what different places were they going on this cruise? 14. When Mrs. Bentham objected to their spending so much money on a cruise, how did Mr. Bentham convince her that they should really go? 15. What is the significance of the title of this story, "Better Late"?

B—Give Sentences with the Following:

to say to oneself
to take a trip
to grow up
to run around
to get into trouble
to make believe
to be *sound* asleep
as far as he was concerned
to make a speech
to pick out
to take care of
to be about to

C—Vocabulary Practice. Answer each of the following correctly:

1. The opposite of *calm,* when referring to the water of the ocean or a lake, is (smooth, windy, rough, pleasant).

2. Which of these do we customarily leave for the waiter after eating in a restaurant (cigarettes, bonus, tip, message)?

3. A common, somewhat slangy, synonym for *children* is (grown-ups, wild-Indians, adults, kids).

4. To *make believe* is to (get seasick, fall asleep, be asleep, pretend).

5. *Sound asleep* means (lightly asleep, deeply asleep, awake, half-asleep).

6. What is the difference in meaning and use between *beside* and *besides?*

7. Which of the following is an adverb: wedding, crazy, golden, awkwardly?

8. What is the past tense form of these verbs: to provide, to feel, to happen, to fly, to do, to breathe?

9. How many syllables are there in the word *advertisement?* In the word *trouble?* In the word *brought?*

10. When I say that I did *pretty* well on my examination, I mean that I did (very well, awfully well, rather well, not well at all).

11. To *mind* something is to (like it, approve of it, insist on it, object to it).

CONHEÇA DO MESMO AUTOR

Robert J. Dixson

Easy Reading Selections in English

For Intermediate Level

With Drills in Conversation Based on the Reading Selections

DISAL EDITORA

Este livro foi impresso na Gráfica Vida e Consciência
sobre papel offset 90g/m² em dezembro de 2007